Rugs & Wall Hangings

Rugs & Wall Hangings

PERIOD DESIGNS AND CONTEMPORARY TECHNIQUES

By JOAN SCOBEY

ORIGINAL DESIGNS AND ILLUSTRATIONS BY
MARJORIE SABLOW

The Dial Press   New York   1974

To Manpa

FIRST PRINTING

Design by Bob Antler

Composition by The Haddon Craftsmen
Printed by Connecticut Printers, Inc.
Bound by Economy Bookbinding Corp.

Foreword

The unsurpassed, richly decorated textiles of the Middle Ages, which had to meet the standards and critical acclaim of Guild Masters, were the result of centuries of fine craftsmanship. The colorful patterned rugs of the Near and Far East, which decorated palaces and temples and in less intricate form were used at every level of society to meet everyday domestic needs, were also the product of several generations of transmitted skills, each family taking pride in the unique patterning of its rugs. However, this special relationship between people and textiles, and between the public and the craftsmen, was radically altered by the Industrial Revolution. Fabrics that had required many hours of patient manual labor were suddenly produced with speed and in large quantities. Elaborate textile fashions and ornamental decorations, once the domain of the prosperous, were within reach of almost every social stratum with patterns and textures reproduced in quantity but lacking individuality. Among the few who tried to move against this overwhelming and, for the manufacturer, profitable industrial tide, were archaeologists, anthropologists, artists, amateur historians, collectors, and craftsmen, all of whom realized that this new, economically advantageous social development carried with it the hazards of conformity which extinguishes creative craftsmanship and interpretation. They began to advocate the collection of pattern drafts and objects. Today, thanks to the efforts of the few within every country, these handmade treasures of the past are displayed with pride in national and private museums as a record of man's artistic and creative history.

It is, therefore, essential that those of us who both enjoy the color and feel of textiles and need to work with our hands turn to our museums and books which study craftsmanship and designs of the past so that we may find in them an inspiration for the present. We must be willing to give the time, the effort, and the concentration required by fine handwork, and commit ourselves to quality of material and design, just as the Guild Masters and craft families did in the past.

In this age of ever-increasing automation and the synthetic copy in everyday life, it is essential that the positive and real link between our children's children and civilization's ancient craftsmen not be lost. I sincerely hope that Joan Scobey's book will play a positive role in the strengthening of this link and continuity of craftsmanship.

Lilo Markrich
The Textile Museum
Washington, D.C.

Acknowledgments

Of the many people who have been helpful to me in my wanderings through the fascinating world of rugs, I want especially to thank the following who generously shared their time, their knowledge, and, in many cases, their valuable photographs.

Bernice Beenhouwer, Sante Fe.

Doris Leslie Blau, New York.

Clarke W. Costikyan and Samuel Proodian of Kent-Costikyan, Inc., New York.

Walter B. Denny, Assistant Professor of Art History, University of Massachusetts, and Honorary Curator of Rugs, Fogg Art Museum, Harvard University.

Grose Evans, Curator of Decorative Arts, National Gallery of Art, Washington, D.C..

David Franses, London.

Lilo Markrich, The Textile Museum, Washington, D.C.

Stanley Reed, Perez, Ltd., London.

Gloria F. Ross and Pace Editions, Inc., New York.

Charles E. Slatkin, New York.

Rexford Stead, Deputy Director, Los Angeles County Museum of Art.

Lina Steele, Index of American Design, National Gallery of Art, Washington, D.C.

Tatu Tuohikorpi, Cultural Attaché, Consulate General of Finland, New York.

Charles Walford, Sotheby & Co., London; and most particularly, John R. Menke, whose passion for scholarship sets an awesome example.

And finally, I want to express my gratitude to all my colleagues at The Dial Press for shepherding the manuscript through the editorial process with care and taste; in particular, to Warren Wallerstein for his loving attention to detail in the production of photographs, art work, and text; to Bob Antler and Paulette Nenner for their imaginative design, and to my editor, Dick Marek, for his enthusiastic support and friendship.

Contents

III. **A PORTFOLIO OF
    DESIGN
    ADAPTATIONS FOR
    RUGS
    AND WALL HANGINGS**   179

Color inserts follow pages 54 and 150

Introduction

Rugs and wall hangings have always been an important part of man's home environment. In the earliest days they were plaited or crudely woven, tacked to walls as shelter from the winds and sun, and laid on the bare ground for warmth and protection against mud, damp, and cold. This is still true in primitive cultures and with nomadic people. But in general as civilizations become more sophisticated and people settle in villages and towns, the artifacts with which they surround themselves become finer and take on aesthetic values in addition to their purely utilitarian ones. In this way rugs became a decorative art form, as truly representative of a culture as its painting, pottery, and jewelry.

Today there is a renewed love of rugs and carpets as an art form, and a resurgence of interest in handmade carpets. People are eager to search out the splendid decorative examples from past cultures, study their designs and techniques, and utilize them to hand-craft their own rugs and hangings.

This book is intended to help you do just that: examine the rugmaking styles and methods of some other cultures and apply them to the most popular contemporary techniques—needlepoint, latch hooking, rya, and punch hooking. You will find a wide diversity of period and contemporary designs, ranging from the bold geometrics of nomadic mideastern tribes and the graceful court arabesques of Persia to the equally striking rya rugs and hangings of Scandinavia and the bold and imaginative styles of the contemporary art market. You will see many photographs of historic and antique rugs and carpets, and find pages of design adaptations ready for you to work.

You will learn how rugs and hangings were made in their own cultures, and by what contemporary technique they can most faithfully be translated. Some period designs can be adapted with complete integrity. The style, texture, and technique of early American hooked rugs, for example, can be reproduced with total fidelity by contemporary punch hooking methods. On the other hand, although the fine pile texture of some Persian and Indian rugs, woven with hundreds of hand-tied knots in each square inch, could never be duplicated without a finely strung loom, you can capture their rich colors and magnificent designs using needlepoint techniques.

Because loom weaving is a complicated and technical craft requiring its own set of design blueprints, the rugmaking methods in this book are arbitrarily limited to needlepoint, latch hooking, rya, and punch hooking. They all rely on hand-held devices or tools, and among them offer more than enough variety of texture and design translation to recreate any of the designs in this book. In addition, most are relatively portable, so today's mobile rugmaker can take a project almost anywhere on the move. Moreover, except for very fine needlepoint, the four methods don't require great manual dexterity or keen eyes, thus extending their appeal to the young, the elderly, the poor sighted, and other would-be craftsmen who fear they are all thumbs.

The design adaptations throughout will suggest typical or characteristic color schemes and rugmaking methods most closely related to the original product. Follow these suggestions if you want to translate a period design with as much fidelity as possible. Don't, however, overlook the possibilities of a free and flexible approach. Be encouraged to make your own adaptations of color, technique, and design so that the rug or hanging you make will truly be your own. Don't hesitate to substitute blue or brown, for instance, in a traditionally red Bokhara if that suits your mood or your décor. Or make a pleasing rya design in needlepoint rather than the traditional Scandinavian stitch. Or adapt a flat-woven Navajo design in the long-pile latch hook technique.

Enjoying and learning from the decorative arts of other people is a visual and spiritual delight. Adapting the designs and riches of other cultures is a superb way of paying tribute to the past and enriching the present. Look to the past for the great designs, and to the present for the rugmaking techniques compatible with contemporary life. By combining both worlds, you will create heirlooms of your own.

Joan Scobey
Westchester, N.Y.

Rugs of Yesterday and Today

Preceding page. Camp Scene by Mir Sayyid Ali, about 1540. A Persian miniature painting illustrating a wide variety of textile motifs as well as some animals and flowers that often appear in hunting and garden carpets. *Photo courtesy Fogg Art Museum, Harvard University, Cambridge, Massachusetts.*

From the East

Among the most prized and popular period rugs are the array of orientals that come to us from the vast reaches of Asia, from the Aegean to the China Sea. They range from the unsophisticated geometrics of Caucasian nomadic tribes to finely detailed hunting scenes of the Persian and Indian courts to the subtly shaded symbolic designs of Imperial China. All beautiful in their own way, these diverse orientals are a legacy of the East, an art form reflecting the varied life styles of the peoples who lived there.

Although the origins of rugmaking are not well documented, they began in the East. Rugs are mentioned in the Old Testament and in Homer. They were known in the Egypt of the Pharaohs and to the ancient Chinese. The earliest-known hand-knotted carpet was discovered by a Russian archeologist in 1949 in southern Siberia, well preserved in ice in the tomb of a Scythian chieftain that dates to 500 B.C. The 2500-year-old carpet is finely knotted, about 6 feet square, and was probably made in East Turkestan, Asia Minor, or Persia.

The discovery of this remarkable carpet inevitably led to the assumption that fine carpetmaking existed in earlier civilizations. Many Greek historians, such as Herodotus and Xenophon, write of carpets in Egypt, Mesopotamia, and the Middle East; and the craft had surely come to Persia during the reign of Cyrus, whose tomb was

3

said to be covered with precious rugs. What is reputed to be the most beautiful carpet of all time—the garden carpet known as the "Spring of Chosroes"—was made in sixth century A.D. Persia during the reign of Chosroes I. The carpet was immense, about 90 feet square, and represented the flowers and streams of a springtime garden, woven in silk and encrusted with clear and colored gemstones to give the illusion of water, flowers, and fruit. It was laid in the royal palace as an indoor garden to delight the Persian ruler during inclement weather. Its beauty and obvious value also delighted the conquering Arabs who carried it away and divided it as their spoils.

For another two thousand years there is very little actual evidence of oriental weaving, except for two rugs found in a mosque in central Turkey which date to the eleventh and twelfth centuries. Other documentary evidence of oriental carpets rests with historians and, by the Renaissance, with painters like Hans Holbein the Younger and Lorenzo Lotto who occasionally depicted them in their work.

By the sixteenth century carpetmaking was well established in Persia and Turkey, and these carpets eventually found their way to Europe via Venice and North Africa. The craft itself spread north to the Caucasus and east to India, Turkestan, and China. Each region has its own history and design characteristics, but the weaving techniques are common to all.

Rugmaking Techniques

Oriental rugs were made by hand on either horizontal or vertical looms. The horizontal looms originated with the nomads who strung warp threads horizontally between two wooden beams which were held in place by posts hammered into the ground. When the nomads broke camp they simply pulled up the posts, rolled the completed part of the carpet and the warp threads around the beams, and moved on.

As the nomads began to settle in villages, they devised a more permanent vertical loom with fixed beams. Here the length of the rug was limited to the height of the loom. In time, a roller beam loom was devised on which could be produced carpet of any length simply by rolling the finished portions onto one of the beams while unrolling additional warp threads from the other beam. Whatever type of loom was used, it was strung with 8 to 60 warps per inch of width, each warp pulled taut between the two main beams. Then the rug was either woven with a flat surface or knotted for a pile texture.

Knotted Rugs. To produce pile rugs, two principal types of knots were used: the Turkish (Ghiordes) and the Persian (Sehna). The Turkish knot is looped around two contiguous warp threads, the Persian knot around only one, making it less bulky and better suited to finely knotted carpets. The type of knot does not indicate the origin of the rug; in fact, the town of Sehna, which gives its name to the Persian knot, often uses the Turkish knot in its weaving. Nor does the type of knot make any difference in quality. These are simply two different methods of tying the yarn around the warp threads.

The weaver works from the bottom of the rug toward the top, sometimes using 2- to 3-inch-long pieces of wool for each knot, sometimes using long strands of yarn. After each knot is tied, the weaver pulls the wool toward him to tighten the knot. When one or more horizontal rows of knots have been tied, one or more weft threads are "shot" from one side to the other, over and under the warp threads, then each weft thread is beaten down against the preceding row to give the fabric density and strength. Sometimes up to four rows of knots are tied before a weft is shot, and sometimes up to six rows of weft are inserted between each row of knots, depending on whether fineness of texture or strength is desired. After every few rows of knots are tied, they are given a preliminary rough cutting. The knotted and weft rows are built up in this way until the textile is completed.

The design of the carpet is indicated in various ways. The Persians often weave a small sample, about 3 by 5 feet, showing all aspects of the pattern, or make an enlarged drawing keying individual knots to separate squares on the graph. The Indians have an elaborate system called *ta'-lem* for transcribing the design; the *ta'lem* writer records the color of each knot row by row and a *ta'lem* reader intones it to a roomful of weavers working at looms. The colors are often noted in code as protection against theft. The Chinese draw a full-sized model of the rug design on paper, and place it behind or beside the loom for weavers to copy, or occasionally trace the design in ink right on the taut warp threads.

When the entire carpet is completed, the final shearing of the pile takes place. The finer the knotting and yarn, the shorter the pile can be cut. Finally the warp threads at each end of the carpet may be knotted for a fringe and the carpet washed and dried in the sun.

The quality of the carpet rests in part on the density of the weave, that is, how close together the knots are tied. This depends on the number of warp threads strung per inch and on the fineness of the yarn used for the warp and the weft. The more knots that are tied in each square inch of carpet, the finer the resulting texture will be. Carpets of extremely fine texture have 400 and more knots per square inch, coarse-textured rugs may have 50 or fewer knots per square inch.

Fineness of texture is only one measure of carpet quality; specimens of beautiful design and workmanship have been woven in coarse textures. The collection of oriental rugs in the Bargello Museum in Florence includes one rug with 700 Persian knots per square inch and another with 58 Turkish knots per square inch. Actually the density of a rug and the length of its pile are closely related to climate, wealth, and life style. The nomadic tribes wove thick, coarse rugs in part because they had little time for fine work, and in part because the rugs were needed not for

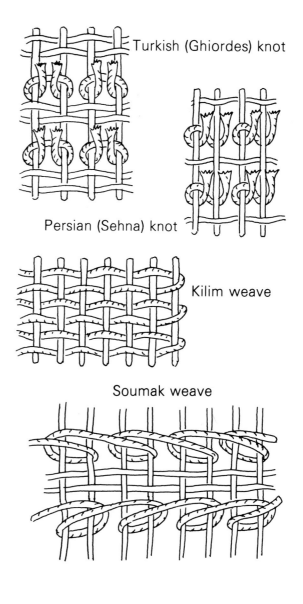

Turkish (Ghiordes) knot

Persian (Sehna) knot

Kilim weave

Soumak weave

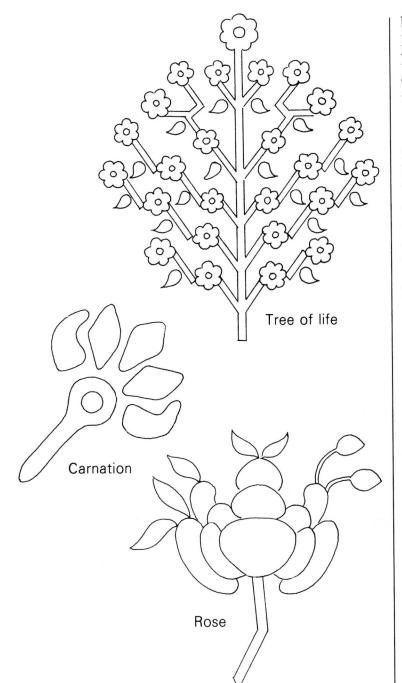

Tree of life

Carnation

Rose

beauty but for protection against the weather. More sophisticated and sedentary villagers, who had more time to produce finely knotted rugs, enjoyed them as much for their beauty as for their utility.

Flat-Woven Rugs. There are various kinds of flat-woven, or nonpile, oriental rugs, the best known of which are the kilim and the Soumak. The kilim, probably the earliest kind of oriental weaving, has a plain weave made by shooting the weft over and under the warp threads in one row, then alternating under and over in the next row. The weft threads always cover the warp and form a selvage on each side. Kilims are made in Turkey, Persia, the Caucasus, and parts of Turkestan.

The Soumak is much coarser than the kilim and is woven in a herringbone pattern by wrapping a continuous weft thread around pairs of warp threads. The weft yarn goes forward over four warps, then back over two warps, then forward over four warps, and so forth. Soumaks are woven throughout the Middle East, particularly in the Caucasus.

Flat-woven rugs are not as durable and sturdy as pile carpets for floor wear, and were often used for door hangings and bed covers. Light in weight and without bulk, the kilims were especially favored by nomads for transporting possessions and furnishing their tents.

In general, flat-woven rugs are made in the same colors and designs as pile rugs from the same region or tribe and are recognized by the same characteristics. However, because of the weaving technique, designs with horizontal or diagonal areas of color were more successful than designs with vertical blocks of color.

Yarns and Dyes

Whether a rug was woven flat or with a pile, the same materials were used in its production. The warp and weft were usually wool or cotton, depending on the region. In pile rugs the knots were almost always sheep's wool; occasionally goat's hair was used in Turkish, Caucasian, and Turkestan rugs; and more rarely, camel's hair. Silk was expensive and found only in fine Persian carpets.

The yarn was colored by dyes extracted from flowers, roots, and insects. Whether the pure color was used alone, or combined in shades and tints, the spectrum was wide and included every color that could be derived from natural dyes— blues, reds, greens, browns, yellows, orange, ivory, beige, white. Oriental weavers also used the natural colors of sheep's wool and camel's hair which did not take dye well. Natural black wool was uncommon, so black coloring, the only nonvegetable dye, was made with vinegar and iron shavings. The black dye sometimes ate the wool away, creating a carved look.

The actual colors themselves often had symbolic as well as decorative importance. Red is the color of joy, life, and many virtues, and thus most popular; blue, the national color of Persia, means solitude; rose or pink connotes divine wisdom; brown, earth and fertility; white is the color of peace as well as mourning and death; black the color of sorrow and evil, and rarely used; green, the sacred color of Mohammedans, represents life and re-birth and thus immortality and is rarely used except in prayer rugs where it is sanctified.

Rug Designs and Characteristics

Oriental carpets are usually classified in regional groups which share similar characteristics of design and color. The major classifications are Persian, Indian, Turkish, Caucasian, Turkoman, Samarkand, and Chinese. Within each region most rugs are further identified either by the village or area of manufacture, by the market place from which they are sold, or by the tribe that produces them.

In general the stylistic treatment of oriental carpets falls broadly into two groups: the elabo-

rate, elegant, and graceful curvilinear designs from Persia and India, many of which are the products of sophisticated court life; and the geometric shapes and patterns from the Caucasus and Turkestan, simpler and cruder in conception and woven by nomadic tribes and village settlers. The rugs of Turkey reflect both styles, but are primarily geometric. Samarkand and Chinese carpets are distinctive in another way, employing a recognizable and unique group of symbols and colors.

Despite the sharp contrasts in styles and distinctive motifs that clearly indicate the origin of a particular rug, many designs are common to diverse regions, spread by the movement of people and trade. The familiar cloud band of China, for example, is also found in Turkish and Persian rugs as is the pear-shaped figure called a *boteh;* the sun wheel, swastika, and tree of life are all ancient symbols used in many areas. Whether expressed geometrically or curvilinearly, flowers of all kinds are beloved in oriental carpets—in full bloom, as rosettes, with leaves, branches, in formalized configurations such as the *herati* pattern. The most popular are carnations, hyacinths, anemones, tulips, lotuses, peonies, roses, palmettes, and also cypress, willow, and poplar trees.

Animals, birds, and insects were also favored motifs, from the realistic and finely detailed elephants, tigers, stags, and antelopes of Persian and Indian hunting carpets to the stylized tarantulas and birds of Caucasian origin. The most popular animals—many of them with symbolic meanings —include the bat, bee, beetle, boar, butterfly, camel, crab, crow, deer, dog, dove, dragon, duck, elephant, fly, hog, lion, magpie, parrot, peacock, phoenix, rooster, scorpion, sparrow, squirrel, stork, tarantula, tiger, and tortoise. Animal figures are noticeably absent in Turkish carpets because Orthodox Mohammedans believe that the Prophet prohibits representations of living creatures.

Common to virtually all types of orientals is the prayer rug; the Moslem always has one at hand on which to perform his five daily prayers.

He spreads it over the ground for cleanliness, with the point of the prayer niche, or *mihrab*, pointing toward Mecca. The *mihrab* actually substitutes for the prayer niche in the Great Mosque at Mecca. The worshipper touches his bowed head to an ornamental stripe or medallion above the *mihrab* and rests his hands on a pair of ornaments on the left and right sides of the rug. Families occasionally pray together on a large rug with multiple *mihrabs*, called a *saph*, but usually each worshipper has his own small rug about 3½ feet by 4½ feet. An essential object in Moslem life, the prayer rug reflects the distinctive design styles of each region. The Persian *mihrab*, for example, is formed by curved lines, the others by straight lines; the Persian and Turkish prayer niches are pointed, the Caucasian and Turkestan often flat on top.

Persian

From the bejewelled beauty of the garden carpet of Chosroes to the silken splendors of the sixteenth and seventeenth centuries, the rugs of Persia are often regarded as the most beautiful in the world. And Persia itself often seems synonymous with the best of oriental weaving.

Historically the long tradition of carpetmaking culminated in the golden age of Persian carpets during the Safavid dynasty when all the Persian arts—architecture, painting, ceramics, miniatures, textiles—flourished, distinguished by superb coloring and detail, skilled technique, and masterful composition and design. After domination by the Seljuk dynasties and then by the Mongols, the first of the Safavid rulers, Shah Ismail I, encouraged a renaissance of the arts at the beginning of the sixteenth century. Carpetmaking centers were created at Tabriz, for a time the capital, at Kashan in central Persia, and at Kirman and Herat (now Afghanistan) in eastern Persia. Carpetmakers, drawing on the themes and symbols of contemporary Persian art, designed rugs for the magnificent court of their new king. The great miniaturists living at the Shah's court supplied cartoons for the carpets, and poets composed texts for ornamental inscriptions.

Ismail's son, Shah Tahmasp succeeded and continued as a great patron of Persian arts. During his reign, which stretched from 1524 to 1576, some of the great hunting and medallion carpets

Garden prayer carpet in silk with flowering trees, cypresses, and birds in four panels intersected by canals with fish. Signed and dated A.D. 1651. 4'7" by 3'8". *Photo courtesy Sotheby & Co., London.*

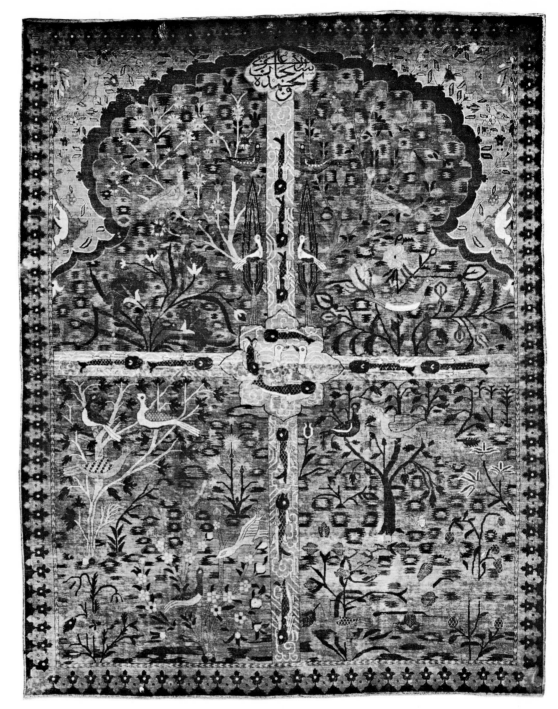

were produced, notably the Ardebil Mosque carpets, regarded by experts as among the most beautiful rugs in existence.

During the reign of Shah Abbas I, carpets of immense size and great beauty were made for palaces and mosques in the workshops at Ispahan, the new capital of Persia. Often incorporating a wide range of color and woven in silk with gold and silver threads, these carpets made splendid gifts to foreign rulers and ambassadors, and introduced Persian carpets to Europe. The death of the great ruler in 1629 ended the golden era of Persian rugs. Toward the end of the seventeenth century, carpetmaking, with the rest of Persian art, declined and the period of court carpetmaking ended when the Afghans invaded Persia in 1722 and destroyed Ispahan.

Court Carpets

Unlike the Persian village carpets which, like other orientals, are classified mainly by their place of origin, the splendid court carpets of the Safavid dynasty are often grouped according to their type of design rather than their place of manufacture.

Garden carpets. Descendants of the Spring of Chosroes, garden carpets are rare and highly prized. In a land where weather ranges from hot and dusty to windy and snowy, the garden is the Persian's personal delight, his cool, green retreat from the harsh climate. Its representation is a cherished design.

Transplanted to rugs, the textile garden was laid out very much like its real-life counterpart. A rectangular plot was often divided by two intersecting paths, creating four flower beds. In larger rugs, as in larger gardens, the paths are grander to accommodate canals, and a shallow pool often marks the central intersection. Trees and flowers may border the avenues, fish or swans may swim in the streams.

Kashan prayer rug design in embossed silk and metal threads. Two flowering trees in shades of brown, pink, wine, and dark blue flank an urn of flowers on a mid-blue field. The main border has palmettes and leaves on a pink ground. 7' by 4'4".
Photo courtesy Sotheby & Co., London.

A detail from the *Coronation Carpet,* a superb animal rug clearly showing its real and legendary animals, birds, and trees. The carpet, so named because it was used in the coronation of King Edward VII, is from northwest Persia, probably Tabriz, and dates from the early 16th century at the beginning of the Safavid dynasty. 23' by 12'. *Photo courtesy Los Angeles County Museum of Art; gift of J. Paul Getty.*

Flower carpets. A variation of the garden carpet is the purely floral rug depicting favorite Persian flowers and trees interconnected with vines and scrolls to completely cover the ground. One version is the Shah Abbas carpet, named for the ruler, and also called an Ispahan because the Shah had established the court manufactory there. The rugs were immense, often more than 50 feet long, and were decorated with large and finely drawn flowers, widely spaced and connected with arabesques.

Vase carpets. Another treatment of the garden carpet is the vase carpet, almost as rare. It is distinguished by the ornamental vases in the design from which spring a profusion of flowers and leafy tendrils so skillfully intertwined that the vases are often hidden among the foliage. Vase carpets are often long and narrow, and usually have a deep red or blue ground.

Animal and hunting carpets. Just as the garden carpets recreated the treasured delights of the Persian garden, so the animal and hunting carpets portrayed the favorite sport of court life. The greatest of these carpets depicted life at the courts of Shah Ismail and Shah Tahmasp. Domestic and wild animals romped or charged amid the blossoms of the lotus and peony, in the shade of the cypress, pomegranate, almond, and magnolia trees. The hunter and his horse stalked a quarry of lions, foxes, jackals, antelopes, ibexes, wild boars, hares, tigers, and panthers, while pheasants and falcons looked on.

Medallion carpets. These are the most typical of Persian court carpets, displaying a large central medallion patterned with flowers and stems and surrounded in the ground by similar arabesques and ornate plants. The motif itself is ancient; it was used in book bindings and illuminated manuscripts long before it was adopted for carpets.

Despite the frequency of the medallion design, the shapes, interior decoration, and surrounding

The *Ardabil Carpet,* one of a pair of celebrated medallion carpets found in the Ardabil Mosque in northwest Persia. Both carpets were signed by Maqsud of Kashan, presumably the master artist-weaver, and dated to correspond with A.D. 1540 during the Safavid dynasty. They are almost identical in design, color, and inscription except that portions of this carpet were used to repair its mate in the Victoria & Albert Museum, London. 23'6" by 13'. *Photo courtesy Los Angeles County Museum of Art; gift of J. Paul Getty.*

Above, an Ispahan prayer rug whose *mihrab*, or prayer niche, is divided into panels, each displaying cloud bands or flower forms. Arabic inscriptions are used in the three borders and outline the *mihrab*. 5'3" by 3'5". *Photo courtesy Perez (London) Ltd.*

Right, a Polish carpet woven in the Persian imperial manufactory during the first half of the 17th century displaying an intricate and symmetrical arrangement of peonies, arabesques, leaves, and tendrils in various shades of blue, orange, and light green on a ground woven of silver threads and chocolate colored silk. 13'2½" by 5'8½". *Photo courtesy the National Gallery of Art, Washington, D.C.; Widener Collection.*

patterns were complex and varied. In early carpets, the medallions were based on 8- or 16-pointed stars, sometimes one inside the other, sometimes with additional star shapes superimposed. Later the medallion evolved into a pear shape, and became more detailed in the interior design and smaller in size.

The most famous of all of these is the Ardebil Mosque Carpet now in the Victoria and Albert Museum in London. Measuring about 17½ feet by 37 feet, with a silk warp and weft, and wool pile, it has about 350 knots in every square inch and it is estimated that it took perhaps ten weavers three and a half years to hand tie its thirty-two million Persian knots. It is signed by the master weaver and dated 946 (1540 A.D.). At the same time, a sister rug was also found in the mosque at Ardebil, a small portion of which was used to repair the London carpet.

Panel carpets. The central field of these rugs are divided into panels of various shapes, each panel framing an animal, bird, or plant.

Polish carpets. These are superbly woven silk carpets so named because they often incorporated the coats of arms of Polish nobles. They were first found in the castles of Poland, either ordered by the nobles from Persia or received as gifts from the shahs during the sixteenth and early seventeenth centuries. Their designs often incorporated palmettes, leaves, arabesques, rosettes, birds, and animals in delicate pastel colors of pale green, orange, light and deep blue, rose, salmon, violet, and brown, all interlaced with gold and silver threads and quite unlike the more familiar Persian rug colors.

Regional and Village Carpets

Hand in hand with the great classic court carpets designed by the most talented artists, executed by the most accomplished weavers in the finest silk and wools are the great variety of fine

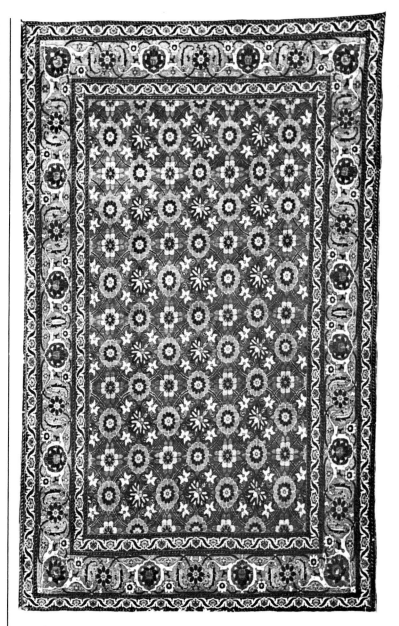

Bakhtiari with an allover *mina khani* motif repeated on the field and framed by a typical border treatment of two narrow guard bands edging a wide central band. 11′ by 7′.
Photo courtesy Perez (London) Ltd.

A rare Bijar rug woven in a Turkish prayer rug design, with a red flower-filled *mihrab*, blue and pink carnation guard stripes, and a broad white border of red and blue poppies. 7'8" by 5'5". *Photo courtesy Sotheby & Co., London.*

regional carpets, produced for centuries by the villagers and tribesmen of Persia. These regional carpets often have common characteristics as well as distinguishing local features. These are among the most popular regional carpets:

Bakhtiari. These have large bold designs which often feature diamond or hexagonal panels in the field, each with a floral or geometric motif. They are coarsely woven with 80 to 120 Turkish knots per square inch.

Bijar. Generally these have floral motifs, sometimes with a central medallion, sometimes with an allover *herati* pattern. Antique Bijars showed a great deal of natural camel's hair in the field; modern Bijars have dark backgrounds of blue, green, and especially red. They are coarsely woven with less than 100 Turkish knots per square inch.

Feraghan. Most common is an allover *herati* pattern on a ground of dark blue or red surrounded by three to nine border stripes. Antique Feraghans are moderately dense with 80 to 200 Persian knots per square inch; modern Feraghans are coarser, with 50 to 160 knots per square inch.

Hamadan. This town is the marketplace for the rugs of many surrounding villages. The rugs frequently have a central hexagonal medallion or a pole medallion whose design is echoed in the four corners. The buff color of natural camel's hair, blue, and red are often used in the borders and background. Hamadans are coarsely woven with 50 to 100 Turkish knots per square inch.

Herez. A common design is a central medallion and floral arabesques treated geometrically on a field of brick red. They are coarsely woven with 50 to 100 Turkish knots per square inch.

Ispahan. Abandoned as a court carpetmaking center after the Afghan occupation in 1722, Ispahan started producing rugs again in the nine-

Left, characteristic Herez with large central medallion predominantly midnight blue and ivory, and other motifs in deep rust, brown, mustard, pale green, and pink. 10′ by 13′. *Photo courtesy Doris Leslie Blau.*

Below, a traditional Ispahan design of flowers and vines surrounding a medallion-like cluster of rosettes and leaves. 7′6″ by 5′. *Photo courtesy Perez (London) Ltd.*

A floral Kashan displaying a large central medallion with finial at top and bottom surrounded by flowers and vines. *Photo courtesy Kent-Costikyan, Inc., New York.*

teenth and twentieth centuries, recreating the traditional designs. These have floral, especially Shah Abbas, patterns, often with a central medallion surrounded with scrolling vines and flowers on a field of deep red or blue. They are densely woven with 150 to 400 Persian knots per square inch.

Kashan. Like Ispahan, Kashan looms lay idle from the Afghan occupation to the late nineteenth century. Typically, Kashans have a central medallion surrounded by densely floral and leafy designs on a brick red or dark blue ground. Also common are pictorial Kashans of silk whose border usually relates a Persian legend and whose field illustrates one of the scenes. They are fairly densely woven with 130 to 350 Persian knots per square inch.

Khorassan. Predominating is an allover *herati* design which originated in this area and was named for its ancient capital, Herat. Also popular is a *boteh* motif. The weaving varies from moderate to fine, with 100 to 350 Persian knots per square inch.

Kirman. Typically these have floral designs, many with central medallions whose motifs are repeated in the corners and border; some rugs have a tree of life. Colors are pastel and delicate, often with an ivory ground. They are finely woven with 200 to 400 Persian knots per square inch.

Kurdistan. Woven by the Kurdish tribes, they frequently have a geometric allover *herati* or *boteh* pattern in dark red, blue, green, and yellow. They are coarsely woven with 50 to 80 Turkish knots per square inch.

Sarouk. One common design is a central medallion with floral decoration, both treated somewhat angularly. Antique Sarouks also use the *boteh* motif. Distinctive colors are dark red, blue, ivory, and a pinkish brick red. They are densely

A pictorial Kashan woven with silk and metal threads in wine, gray, purple, and blue on a silver field. 6′ by 4′2″.
Photo courtesy Sotheby & Co., London.

Left, Khorassan with a rare and interesting interpretation of a tree of life.
8′2″ by 5′11″. *Photo courtesy Kent-Costikyan, Inc., New York.*

Right, another unusual use of tree forms in a Kirman with flowers both filling and surrounding cypress trees on a prayer niche supported by two columns. 7′ by 4′10″. *Photo courtesy Perez (London) Ltd.*

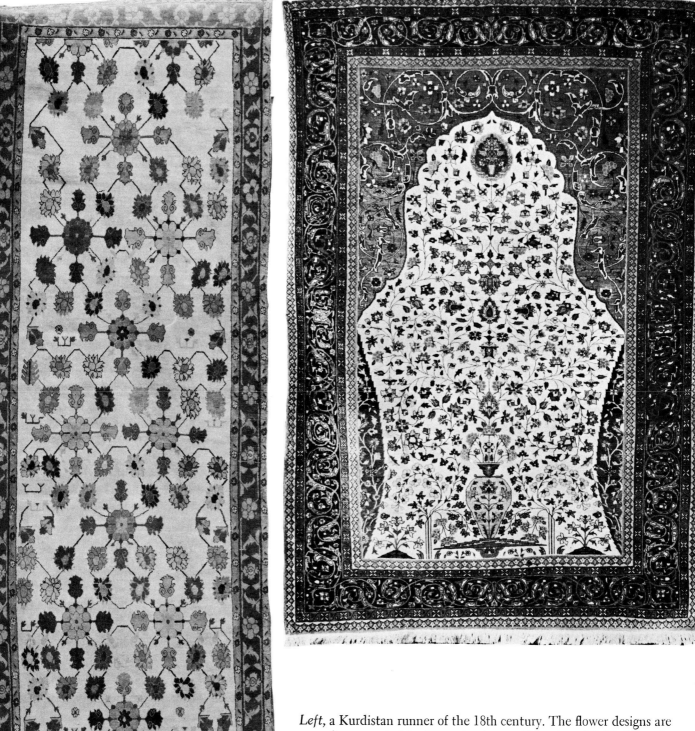

Left, a Kurdistan runner of the 18th century. The flower designs are often repeated in different colors on the oatmeal field; the main floral border is pink. 14'11" by 3'6". *Photo courtesy Sotheby & Co., London.*

Right, a Sarouk prayer rug whose well-foliated *mihrab* includes a charming decorative vase. 6'9" by 4'7". *Photo courtesy Perez (London) Ltd.*

Two treatments of an allover *boteh* motif. In the Sehna, *left*, the flower-filled *botehs* face the same direction on a flower- and leaf-filled ground; in the Sarabend, *right*, the rows of ornamental *botehs* alternately face right and left and are set against a plain dark field. The Sehna is 6'6" by 4'6"; the Sarabend is 5' by 2'7". *Photo at left courtesy Kent-Costikyan, Inc., New York; right, courtesy Perez (London) Ltd.*

woven with 160 to 400 Persian knots per square inch.

Sehna. These rugs often have a central diamond or pole medallion, or an allover *herati* or *boteh* design. Colors are subdued: dark blue and wine, light ivory and yellow. They are densely woven, with from 200 to 500 and more Turkish knots per square inch.

Sarabend. A typical design has rows of *botehs*, often facing left in one row and right in the next, fitted closely together to fill a dark blue or red field. They are moderately woven with 100 to 150 Turkish knots per square inch.

Shiraz. Untypically geometric Persians, these have single-pole medallions or diamond-shaped lozenges in the center or repeated two or three times along the length of the carpet, usually in light or dark blue on a red field decorated with plant forms. They are moderately woven with about 100 Persian or Turkish knots per square inch.

Tabriz. Also known for its prayer rugs, this region produces carpets that often have a central medallion with large floral motifs of leaves and stems and occasionally a tree of life design. They are finely woven with 150 to 400 Turkish knots per square inch.

Design

Whether treated in the graceful and flowing style we think of as typically Persian, or in the angular treatment that occurs in some western sections of the country, certain motifs appear again and again.

Herati. In its simplest form, two elongated leaves encircle a rosette. When used as a repeat pattern, it includes a diamond enclosing a small rosette and surrounded by four of the simple

A handsome Shiraz of unusually fine weave with characteristic geometric diamond-shaped central lozenge in ivory on a midnight blue field filled with flowers. 4'6" by 7'6".
Photo courtesy Doris Leslie Blau.

Left, a late 19th-century Tabriz with central medallion on a soft cinnamon colored ground. The floral motifs are typically large. 4'2" by 6'8". *Photo courtesy Doris Leslie Blau.*

Right, section of an 18th-century runner from northwest Persia showing elaborate forms of the palmette. The flowers are rust, yellow, and dark blue on a turquoise field bordered with a simple vine and flower band. 13'5" by 4'5". *Photo courtesy Sotheby & Co., London.*

herati figures. It is often used as a border motif.

Boteh. This is a pear-shaped figure, also known as the cone pattern, often filled with interior decorations. The *boteh* is usually small, between 2 and 8 inches long, and set in diagonal or perpendicular lines over the entire field, or used as a border motif. It is the forerunner of the paisley pattern.

Mina Khani. This is a diamond enclosing a rosette with four larger flowers at each point. As a repeat, each figure is connected with curving stems to form a diaper pattern.

Shah Abbas. A floral pattern including various elaborate forms of the palmette used alone in a field or border and connected with vines. The flowers are often yellow, red, and blue on a blue background. The pattern, named for the Persian ruler, occurs often in Ispahan rugs.

Medallions. Often based on an 8- or 16-pointed figure, they may be square, oval, round, or diamond-shaped. A quarter of the central medallion may be repeated in each corner.

Pole medallion. A medallion with rod-like extensions often leading to smaller medallions.

Tree of life. Occurs in many variations.

Flowers. A large variety from the Persian garden, including narcissi, roses, zinnias, asters, balsams, chrysanthemums, marigolds, portulacas, cockscombs, dahlias, larkspurs, sweet williams, pinks, tulips, violets, lilies, pansies, petunias, irises, and lilacs.

Animals. Stags, horses, dogs, lions, foxes, jackals, antelopes, ibexes, boars, hares, tigers, panthers, monkeys, and deer.

Birds. Peacocks, parrots, pheasants, and falcons.

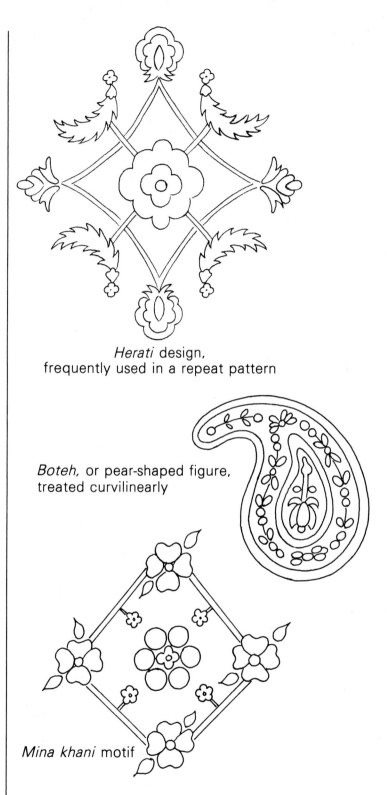

Herati design, frequently used in a repeat pattern

Boteh, or pear-shaped figure, treated curvilinearly

Mina khani motif

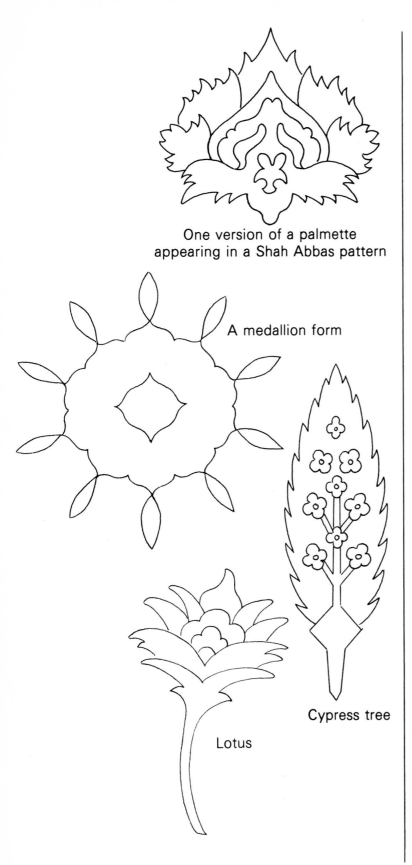

One version of a palmette
appearing in a Shah Abbas pattern

A medallion form

Cypress tree

Lotus

Borders are predominantly floral, with individual flowers in infinite variations often contained within a winding S-shaped vine. Rows of *botehs* are common, with the figures laid horizontally or at an angle.

Color

Much of the beauty of Persian rugs comes from the masterful use of color, used alone and combined in shades and tints. Basic were blue, the national color of Persia, red, green, brown, yellow, orange, ivory, and beige, as well as the natural colors of sheep's wool and camel's hair.

Rugmaking Technique

Most Persian rugs use the Persian knot, although the Turkish knot is occasionally found, especially in rugs made in the western section of the country bordering Turkey. Flat-woven kilims are also made in Persia, particularly around Sehna.

Wool and cotton are most commonly used for the warp and weft. The pile is usually tied with wool, since sheep were raised all over the country, occasionally with camel's hair, and only rarely with silk.

To approximate the pile texture, use Turkey tufting on needlepoint canvas *(see* Chapter 17) or latch hooking *(see* Chapter 18).

To approximate the flat texture of a kilim, use the Gobelin or Soumak stitch on needlepoint canvas *(see* Chapter 17).

Indian

India, which produced some of the greatest carpets in the world, never really developed a style one could call characteristically Indian. The skills, the designs, even the weavers, were originally imported from Persia, and a carpet industry sprang into instant production. Even after a hundred years of making breathtakingly beautiful carpets, it is curious that Indian rugs never took on an independent native flavor but essentially remained a stepchild of Persia.

India owed its golden century of rugmaking to three generations of Mogul emperors who ruled from the middle of the sixteenth century to the middle of the seventeenth century—Akbar, Jahangir, and Shah Jahan, best known for building the Taj Mahal. Akbar was a progressive and reform-minded ruler, and although he himself was illiterate, his courts were centers of learning. In an attempt to introduce high quality rug production to India, he turned to the example set by his contemporary, Shah Abbas, in neighboring Persia. Under the supervision of Persian weavers, Akbar set up royal looms at Lahore, then later at Agra, Delhi, and other cities. Rug weaving soon became so popular that nobles paid particularly good weavers to live and work at their homes.

The Indian rugs produced on the royal looms were all modeled after Persian carpets, and found their greatest expression in floral designs and hunting and animal carpets. Many of Akbar's

Opposite page, magnificent Mogul animal carpet woven in the imperial Indian manufactory about 1630 and depicting an elephant and his rider walking through a forest, a rhinoceros chasing a deer, a crocodile confronting a winged lion, two giraffes in combat, and gazelles, deer, and other animals running amid leaves and flowers on the pale claret ground of the carpet. The detail, above, shows a dragon catching a goat, a tiger and leopard fighting, and a winged lion. 13'3" by 6'3¼". *Both photos courtesy National Gallery of Art, Washington, D.C.; Widener Collection.*

rugs were made for his huge harem and for the large new palace of Fathpur, the Versailles he built to honor the birth of his son, Jahangir. Many of the flower rugs are of silk; and the animal and bird carpets tell the stories of his hunting exploits.

After Akbar's death, the weaving of court rugs continued through the reigns of his son and grandson. But when the Mogul Empire was overthrown, production of fine rugs stopped as abruptly as it had begun, primarily because it had been supported by royal patronage. Other factors contributed to the general decline of quality rugmaking in India. The East India Company exported the great rugs and encouraged an era of salable, rather than quality, carpetmaking. Rugs began to be woven by prisoners in jails for low wages, which drove the regular rug weavers out of business. In the twentieth century, however, rugmaking was revived in weaving centers in northern India where men and boys, following principally Persian designs, are making rugs of good quality.

Design

Designs show a strong Persian influence, although the motifs themselves are treated more literally, naturalistically, and symmetrically.

Flowers. Single flowers are shown clearly, including the roots, sometimes in rows, set within a frame or panel, or in a trellis as if climbing.

Animals. There is a literal treatment of native and mythical animals: elephants, leopards, gazelles, giraffes, crocodiles, dragons, goats, rhinoceroses, tigers, and lions.

Color

The Indian palette echoed the Persian, using blues, red, greens, browns, yellows, orange, ivory,

Mogul flower carpet of the 17th century with clearly defined carnations, irises, and lilies in pale pink, yellow, white, and green on a wine field and a *herati* design border in the same colors. 14' by 6'7". *Photo courtesy Sotheby & Co., London.*

Stag

and beige, and frequent use of pink for contrast and outline. The shades of colors in Indian rugs were often lighter than those in Persian.

Rugmaking Technique

Indian pile rugs were densely woven with the Persian knot, commonly having 400 knots per square inch and sometimes 700 to 1,000 in really fine examples. Both wool and silk were used for knotting, with silk rugs more prevalent during the reign of Shah Jahan.

It is not feasible to produce by hand the fine pile texture of the great Indian rugs, but you can capture their intricate designs with the basket-weave or Gobelin stitch on needlepoint canvas *(see* Chapter 17).

Turkish

Of the two early centers of oriental rugmaking, Persia and Turkey, it was the Turkish carpet—or what came to be called the Turkish carpet—that was first known in the West and more strongly influenced European rug design.

Turkish carpets were the first to be imported into Europe. Because of its geographic situation, Turkey was the eastern market place for Europe. From there, oriental rugs, most of them Turkish, were shipped to Venice and then to northern Europe. These Turkish rugs were prized by their western owners and often displayed on tables in the fashion of the period. They were at least common enough to be recorded in the works of various painters during the sixteenth and seventeenth centuries. Hans Holbein the Younger so frequently painted a particular type of Turkish carpet that it came to be called a "Holbein." The design of these Holbeins usually alternated octagonal and diamond forms with geometric arabesques, often bordered with Kufic script, all of which suggested they came from Oushak. Similar carpets appear in the paintings of Lorenzo Lotto, Jan van Eyck, and other Flemish and Italian painters. Obviously, oriental carpets were known in the West, and whatever their actual place of origin, they were generally referred to as Turkish carpets in the same way that hand-knotted pile upholstery fabric was called "Turkey work."

Actually, carpets had been made for centuries

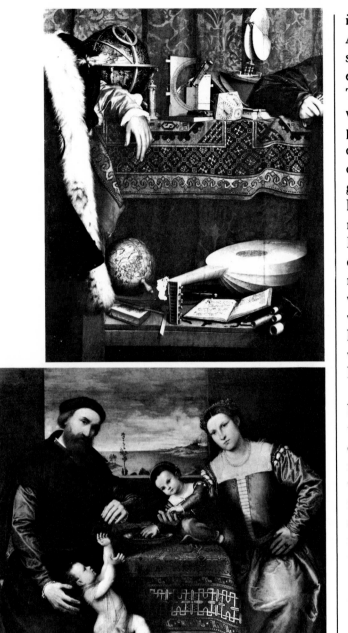

Turkish carpets, highly prized in Europe and often used as table coverings, occasionally appeared in the works of some 16th-century painters. *Top*, a detail of "The Ambassadors" by Hans Holbein the Younger; *above*, "Family Group" by Lorenzo Lotto. *Both photos courtesy the Trustees, The National Gallery, London.*

in Anatolia (the portion of Turkey that lies in Asia Minor) in characteristically geometric designs. The essentially linear treatment was softened by the Persian influences introduced into Turkey by Suleiman the Magnificent. Suleiman, who brought the Ottoman Empire to its greatest power, was a lavish patron of the arts. During an occupation of Persia during the middle sixteenth century, he brought back weavers schooled in the great Persian court style to work at the royal looms in Constantinople. The resulting court rugs of Turkey were a remarkable marriage of Persian palmettes and motifs with Turkish flowers, often surrounding a central medallion. The rugs were finely textured and brightly colored with blues, greens, and golds on a red field. They were often made of silk and tied with the Persian knot unlike the Turkish village carpets which were made in wool and tied with the Turkish knot.

The Persian medallion motif was also adopted by the weavers at Oushak, who interpreted it through the more geometric and stylized shapes of Asia Minor. Gradually the medallion became more complex and later gew into a star shape which gave the name, Star Oushak, to one famous type of carpet made in the sixteenth and seventeenth centuries. The star motif often has four or eight points, and is in blue or yellow repeated on a red or blue field.

The better known carpets of Turkey, however, are the prayer rugs which were woven all over the country for the personal religious use of observant Mohammedans. They are numerous because Islamic precepts are strictly observed in Asia Minor. As they are used most often for individual worship they are usually small, about 4 feet by 6 or 7 feet.

Prayer rugs from different areas can often be recognized by the distinctive shapes of their *mihrabs*, or prayer niches. Most Turkish *mihrabs* have pointed arches, sometimes stepped, and only rarely with a flat top or oval shape. Sometimes the *mihrab* has arches at both ends of the rug; on a family prayer carpet the *mihrab* is often

Top, a silk Anatolian *saph,* or multiple prayer rug, in which each of the nine prayer niches has a different shape and design. 9'8" by 3'4". *Photo courtesy Perez (London) Ltd. Left,* one of the celebrated Star Oushak rugs made in the 16th century, with large octagonal blue stars filled with arabesques on a red field and a cloud band motif in the blue border. 13'5" by 7'5". *Photo courtesy Victoria and Albert Museum, Crown Copyright, London. Above,* a Bergama displaying characteristic design motifs of rectangles, polygons, all fairly large in scale. 4'5" by 3'7". *Photo courtesy Sotheby & Co., London.*

Antique Ghiordes prayer rug with a bouquet of flowers in place of the usual mosque lamp at the point of the plain-colored *mihrab*. The main border has a typical twin rosette and leaf motif and is flanked on either side by floral guard bands. 6′ by 4′4″. *Photo courtesy Sotheby & Co., London.*

repeated once for each member of the family. The *mihrab* field may be left empty or ornamented with a hanging lamp, candlesticks, or other articles from an actual mosque. The surrounding borders usually contain flowers and curving plants, either stylized or realistically treated.

While sharing many of the same general characteristics, the rugs of Turkey, like other oriental carpets, also have regional features.

Bergama. These differ from most other Turkish carpets in that there are fewer prayer rugs, and the typical shape is almost square, rather than rectangular. Rectangles and polygons in various sizes are frequent, sometimes as central medallions and sometimes in a repeat design. The pattern is usually fairly large in proportion to the size of the carpet. Principal colors are red and blue, with motifs in lighter blue, white, orange. The weave is moderate, with 50 to 150 Turkish knots per square inch, and the pile fairly long.

Ghiordes. These great Turkish prayer rugs are characterized by free-standing columns supporting the prayer niche, in which a lamp often hangs at the point. The *mihrab* is often otherwise plain, in ivory or red, surrounded by multiple borders of fine flower patterns and scrolls. The coloring of the rug is usually light: ivory and white, with red, blue, and yellow. The weave is moderate, with 65 to 150 Turkish knots per square inch.

Hereke. This is the site of a royal carpet manufactory staffed with Persian weavers that flourished in the ninteenth century. It produced beautiful silk carpets of essentially Persian design: allover floral patterns typical of Kirman in pastel colors with metallic threads. The weave is very fine.

Konya. These prayer rugs often have a wide *mihrab* with a comparatively shallow stepped gable and stylized flowers above. Columns or a

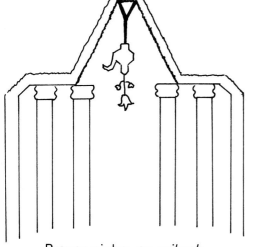

Prayer niche, or *mihrab,*
of a Ghiordes prayer rug

Left, a silk Hereke prayer rug after a Persian design, incorporating cloud bands and flowers in the *mihrab* and leaves growing out of urns in the panel above. 5′ by 3′9″. *Photo courtesy Perez (London) Ltd. and Sotheby & Co., London.*

Right, an unusual Konya prayer rug, about 1800. 5′7″ by 3′9″. *Photo courtesy Kent-Costikyan, Inc., New York.*

Kula prayer rug with garlands of leaves and flowers hanging from the point of the *mihrab*, six peony blossoms on the frieze overhead, and many narrow flower-dotted borders. 5'8" by 4'. *Photo courtesy Perez (London) Ltd. and Sotheby & Co., London.*

hanging lamp may decorate the red or blue *mihrab* field. Geometric borders often use yellow, green, and white. The weave is coarse, 40 to 80 Turkish knots per square inch.

Kula. These prayer rugs have densely decorated *mihrabs*, sometimes with a tree of life, sometimes with two columns flanking garlands of leaves and flowers that foliate the field. In one type of prayer rug, called a cemetery, tomb or grave rug, the *mihrab* is filled with small repeat panels of house-and-cypress-tree motifs. Predominant colors are red, muddy yellow, and blue. They are coarsely woven with 50 to 100 Turkish knots per square inch.

Ladik. Among the best-known and most beautiful Turkish prayer rugs, these are characterized by an odd number of tulips, usually three or five, on stylized stalks either above or below the *mihrab* which commonly has a plain bright red ground. Blues, greens, gold, yellow, and white are frequently used. The weave is moderate, with 64 to 130 Turkish knots per square inch.

Mudjar. These are mainly prayer rugs with a distinctive *mihrab*, stepped and topped with a geometrically figured pole, and surrounded with wide borders. The *mihrab* field is usually deep red, the colorful geometric border motifs in yellow, violet, orange, ivory. The weave is moderately coarse, with 40 to 100 Turkish knots per square inch.

Oushak. Not to be confused with the fine rugs of the sixteenth, seventeenth and eighteenth centuries, contemporary Oushaks generally have a large medallion on a plain red ground. They are coarsely woven with 16 to 60 Turkish knots per square inch.

Yuruk. These are the bulk of Anatolian carpets made by the nomads in the southeast. They have a geometric, Caucasian look, with diamond medallions often encircled by latch hook orna-

Ladik prayer rug of the late 18th century. Five blue tulips hang upside down in the red panel below the triple arched beige *mihrab*; the upper cross panel is beige, the main border is blue. 5′8″ by 3′9″. *Photo courtesy Sotheby & Co., London.*

Stylized tulip typical of a Ladik prayer rug

Left, a Mudjar prayer rug with steeply stepped *mihrab* gable outlined in four colors. The wide lozenge borders are typical. 6'1" by 4'3".
Photo courtesy Perez (London) Ltd. and Sotheby & Co., London.

Right, a "Lotto" Oushak, so called because the design of the main field resembles the rugs painted by the Italian artist (see Lotto's "Family Group" on page 32). Yellow figures with blue on a red field. 8'6" by 5'4".
Photo courtesy Sotheby & Co., London.

Opposite page, Yuruk rug with typical geometric forms and a main border using eight-point stars. 6'7" by 4'5". *Photo courtesy Sotheby & Co., London.*

ments. The colors are unusual: yellow and violet, with some orange, green, and dark blue. The weave is moderately coarse, with 36 to 100 Turkish knots per square inch.

Design

Turkish designs owe much to Persia on the one hand and to the Caucasus on the other, often seeming to meld the curvilinear floral arabesques of the former with the geometric shapes and strong colors of the latter to produce a style that is truly Turkish rather than purely derivative.

Since Moslems believe that the Koran forbids the representation of living creatures, Turkish rugs rarely include human or animal figures, relying instead on such geometric forms as the star, the diamond and other polygons, and on plants and flowers such as tulips, carnations, and hyacinths. Even the well-known bird motif of Anatolia is actually an arrangement of stylized leaves.

Turkish borders also show the same blend of angular and flowing lines, using as popular motifs rosettes and leaves, diamonds and stars, angular scrolls, and a Kufic border based on a tracery-like pattern of calligraphy.

Color

The colors in Turkish rugs are often brighter and richer than those in other oriental carpets. Red, blue, and yellow frequently appear, and to a lesser degree, ivory, orange, violet, and other shades. Green was regarded as a sacred color and used primarily in prayer rugs where it was sanctified.

Rugmaking Technique

Except for the court carpets often made of silk and tied with the Persian knot, all Turkish pile

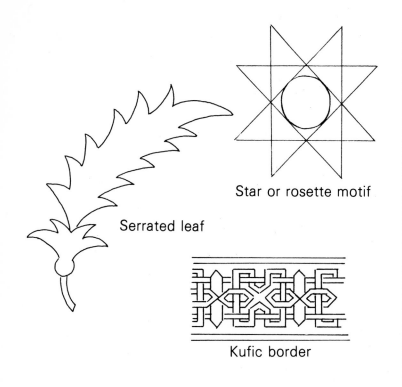

Serrated leaf

Star or rosette motif

Kufic border

rugs are tied with wool in the Turkish knot in a moderately coarse weave.

Reproduce the pile texture of Turkish rugs with Turkey tufting on needlepoint canvas (*see* Chapter 17) or latch hooking (*see* Chapter 18).

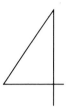

Caucasian

Caucasian rugs are wholly the product of the various tribes inhabiting the wild and mountainous district between the Black and Caspian seas. There was no regulated weaving industry nor court manufactory in the Caucasus as there was in Persia, India, and Turkey. Consequently the rugs are the unsophisticated folk art of the people who live in this rugged region—bold, bright, colorful, and vigorous. Their purely private use combined with the lack of official supervision accounts for the fact that, in general, existing rugs date only from the last half of the eighteenth century.

The only evidences of earlier rugmaking are the Armenian dragon carpets of the fifteenth and sixteenth centuries, probably made at Kuba. Highly stylized in design, they revived an ancient dragon pattern from Asia Minor and combined it with Persian flowers, leaves, and palmettes. The dragon took various forms, sometimes juxtaposed with a phoenix or other animals and birds. These rugs were opulent and formal, quite different from their Anatolian and Persian origins as well as from the better-known and cruder Caucasians.

The Caucasus now comprises several Soviet states, but until the early nineteenth century it belonged to Persia. It is the home of many diverse tribes and two main religions—Christianity and Islam. But despite the change of sovereignty,

41

An Armenian dragon
carpet with stylized
flowers, leaves, and
palmettes of Persian
origin. *Photo courtesy
Sotheby & Co., London.*

the mix of customs, tribes, and many separate languages, Caucasian rugs are remarkably uniform in style and tone.

Most Caucasian carpets use bold, almost primitive, geometric forms, most are bright and colorful, most are small. Some designs are too similar to have distinguishing tribal or village characteristics. Their style is wholly geometric; the curvilinear treatment developed to such a high art in neighboring Persia did not influence Caucasian weavers, perhaps because this rugged region was not easily accessible. Many motifs, however, were taken from Persia and Turkey to be rendered in the virile, linear style of the Caucasus.

These are some of the best-known Caucasian rugs:

Baku. These have large rectilinear *botehs* arranged in rows on a field on which may also appear one or more octagonal medallions. They are woven in untypically dull colors: blues, brown, tan, cream, ivory, and yellow. The weave is fairly coarse, with 42 to 100 Turkish knots per square inch.

Chichi. Small allover mosaic of rosettes or rows of octagons crowded on a blue or red field. The series of wide borders are more important to the design than the field. The rugs are small, 2 to 3 feet by 5 to 5½ feet, with a moderate weave of 60 to 120 Turkish knots per square inch.

Daghestan. This district and its capital Derbent produce rugs that often have stripes across the field and a border decorated with small geometric motifs like squares with hooked ends. Daghestan prayer rugs have angular six-sided *mihrabs* and fields densely covered with a diamond trellis pattern. Principal colors are blue, yellow, and white. The weave is fairly coarse, with 50 to 100 Turkish knots per square inch.

Kabistan. A variety of Daghestan rugs closely related to Kubas, these are often long nar-

Baku with large rectilinear *botehs* surrounding the central geometric medallion. The rosettes and diagonal stripes are typical borders. 6′3″ by 4′5″. *Photo courtesy Sotheby & Co., London.*

Left, characteristic Chichi rug with rows of stylized flower heads on a small field surrounded by many borders, including the typical diagonal band-and-rosette. 6′ by 4′1″.

Right, a Daghestan prayer rug with its angular six-sided *mihrab* gable and field covered with a diamond trellis pattern. The stylized leaf main border is characteristic. 5′6″ by 3′7″.

Both photos courtesy Sotheby & Co., London.

Left, a Kabistan of unusually fine weave with birds, animals, flowers, and human
figures charmingly decorating an indigo blue field. 4′6″ by 3′9″.
Photo courtesy Sotheby & Co., London.

Right, a more elegant treatment of birds in a Karabagh *kelleye,* or long runner,
incorporating the rare and highly prized parrot figures. It is similar but not
identical to the Karabagh in the color section. 15′3″ by 6′4″.
Photo courtesy Perez (London) Ltd.

A Kazak with the well-known sunburst medallion, also called an eagle or *adler* Kazak. The wide-armed cross is decorated with flowers and repeated the length of the field. The typical border links eight-point stars in the "tarantula" pattern. *Photo courtesy Perez (London) Ltd.*

row runners displaying a ram's horn motif on a blue field. Other design elements include rosettes, arabesques, Kufic borders, and *botehs*. Another pattern uses diagonal stripes with small geometric figures. Principal colors are blue, with red, ivory, green, and brown. They are fairly coarsely woven with 50 to 120 Turkish knots per square inch.

Karabagh.   Quite different from other Caucasian carpets, these are largely floral rugs influenced by Persian and even French design, often displaying the *herati* pattern and large bouquets on a magenta field. The weave is moderately dense, with 60 to 160 Turkish knots per square inch.

Kazak.   The best-known and most popular of Caucasian rugs, their geometric pattern is large and bold, often showing more empty ground than other Caucasian carpets. Well-known designs include the sunburst, or *adler*, a cross with two equal arms ending in points and decorated with floral motifs, and one or more large octagonal medallions sometimes encircled by protruding latch hooks. The colors are also bold: red, green, blue, brown, white. The weave is fairly coarse, with 50 to 100 Turkish knots per square inch.

Kuba.   Almost indistinguishable from Kabistans, these are generally long carpets well filled with designs such as medallions with flower shapes, octagons, radiating star forms, and Kufic borders. Main colors are a blue ground, with red, white, some yellow, light blue, and green. The weave is fairly coarse, with 40 to 100 Turkish knots per square inch.

Shirvan.   These carpets from the southern Caucasus are similar to Daghestans, Kubas, and Kabistans and employ a variety of patterns: octagonal medallions sometimes incorporating eight-point stars or latch hooks; large-scale angular florals; small geometric motifs including stars,

A Kuba with three closely grouped geometric medallions decorated with Caucasian motifs. The main border has the diagonally striped barber pole design, the outer border a band of rosettes. 6'2" by 3'6". *Photo courtesy Kent-Costikyan, Inc., New York.*

A classical Shirvan whose well-decorated field has stylized flower heads surrounded by latch hooks, peacocks, and other angular motifs. *Photo courtesy Sotheby & Co., London.*

A Soumak rug woven about 1800 in the identifying flat weave displays a variety of geometric Caucasian motifs, many bordered by latch hooks. The multiple borders have eight-point stars, rosettes, and the running latch hook design. 9'7'' by 6'1''. *Photo courtesy Kent-Costikyan, Inc., New York.*

crosses, and animals. Principal colors are blue, red, yellow, and ivory. The weave is moderately dense, with 60 to 160 Turkish knots per square inch.

Soumak. The principal flat-weave rugs of the Caucasus, they are woven in a herringbone pattern a little more textured than kilims. Their designs are typically Caucasian; one characteristic pattern uses three or more large elongated diamond medallions running across the width of the field, heavily decorated inside and outside the jewel-like polygons. Main colors are blues, soft brick red, yellow, white.

Design

Caucasian design elements are essentially geometric: squares, hexagons, octagons, diamonds, eight-pointed stars, crosses, frets, and latch hooks, all used in large medallions and in small motifs. Even those designs not intrinsically geometric, like flowers, trees, plants, *botehs*, and animals, are treated angularly.

Borders are usually wide and multiple. Their patterns include the latch hook, barber pole, serrated-edge leaf, Kufic script, crab and serpent forms, dots and dashes, posts and bars, stars, small medallions.

Color

Caucasian colors are bold and clear blues, browns, yellows, greens, ivory. Less red is used than in Turkish rugs.

Rugmaking Technique

Except for flat-woven Soumaks, all Caucasian rugs are fairly coarsely woven and tied with the Turkish knot. The warp, weft, and pile are virtually always made of wool, undoubtedly because

The popular *boteh* motif is always treated geometrically in Caucasian rugs. In this Kazak the individual interior decoration of each of the 58 figures lends interest to the repeat pattern. 10' by 4'8". *Photo courtesy Perez (London) Ltd.*

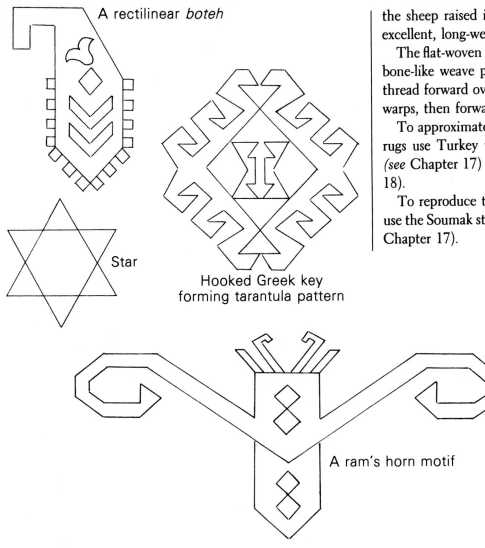

A rectilinear *boteh*

Star

Hooked Greek key
forming tarantula pattern

A ram's horn motif

the sheep raised in the mountainous land yield excellent, long-wearing, and hardy wool.

The flat-woven Soumaks are made in a herringbone-like weave produced by bringing the weft thread forward over 4 warps, then back under 2 warps, then forward over 4 more warps.

To approximate the pile texture of Caucasian rugs use Turkey tufting on needlepoint canvas (*see* Chapter 17) or latch hooking (*see* Chapter 18).

To reproduce the flat weave of Soumak rugs, use the Soumak stitch on needlepoint canvas (*see* Chapter 17).

Turkoman

Rugs from central Asia are known by various names. Afghan and Beluchi refer to the nomad tribes who weave them, Bokhara to a collection and market place, and Turkestan to a large and geographically varied region now in Russia where carpets were made. Collectively they are sometimes classified as Turkoman rugs.

Turkoman rugs are made entirely by the nomads who roam this generally barren area of Asia, from the Caspian Sea east to Chinese Turkestan, from Siberia south through Afghanistan, parts of Persia, and Beluchistan (now in West Pakistan). The men tend their flocks of sheep, goats, and camels, then shear the wool for their rugs. The women weave, producing large rugs to cover the tent floor, small prayer rugs, weavings for pillows, blankets, door hangings, and saddle and tent bags in which to house the paraphernalia of their nomadic life. For protection they weave pile rugs; for utility, flat-woven kilims which are light, strong, and require much less wool than pile fabrics.

Historically Turkoman carpets must have been made for centuries. The trade route from China to Constantinople passed through Central Asia, surely bringing the ancient wares of both the East and the Middle East to the attention of the nomadic tribes. But because there was little contact with the West, Turkoman rugs were not known until the late nineteenth century when

Two Turkoman prayer rugs. *Left,* an Afghan with its identifying tribal *guls* and pear border. 3′9″ by 2′6″. *Photo courtesy Perez (London)* Ltd. *and* Sotheby & Co., *London.*

Right, a Beluchi with a typically stylized tree of life. 4′6″ by 2′7″. *Photo courtesy Sotheby & Co., London.*

the Russians conquered western Turkestan.

This geographic and cultural isolation probably accounts for the distinctive character of Turkoman rugs. In color and design the rugs of many tribes are curiously similar. Most have reddish backgrounds, are geometric compostions, and incorporate in an allover pattern the *gul*, or coat of arms, of the tribe. These are the best known Turkoman rugs:

Afghan. Also known as Khiva Bokhara, these have rows of large octagonal *guls* dominating the field. Inside each *gul* is a smaller octagon or rectangle, with the remainder of the *gul* divided into four sections decorated with the same design in reverse colors. The *guls* are separated by stylized branches and enclosed in a multibanded border. The rugs have a rich red background, the design is in blue, dark brown, or black. The weave is moderately fine, with 60 to 160 Persian knots per square inch.

Beluchi. These are quite different from other Turkoman rugs in that there are no *guls* in the design which typically includes geometric medallions with latch hooks, and prayer rugs with a tree of life. The main colors are red, blue, and light brown, the color of natural camel's hair. The weave is fairly coarse, with 60 to 100 Persian knots per square inch.

Bokhara. This is a name given to many types of carpets collected in this town, the best known of which is made by the Tekke tribe and called the Royal Bokhara. On the typically red field are rows of the distinctive Tekke *gul* alternating with small diamonds. The slightly curved and flattened octagonal *gul* is quartered by vertical and horizontal lines covering the entire field and intersecting at the center of each *gul*. The interior of each *gul* is decorated with leaves and gargoyles within a smaller eight-pointed form with opposing quarters woven in the same colors. The field is always a warm brick red, the designs in blue, black, yellow.

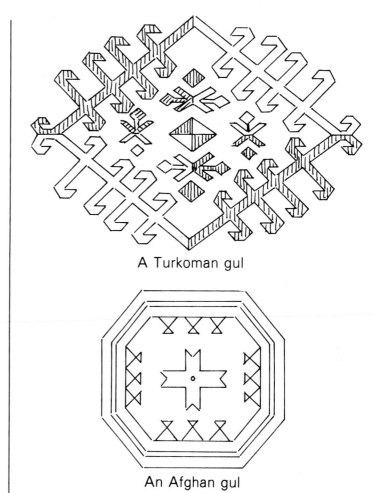

A Turkoman gul

An Afghan gul

Left, a typical Royal Bokhara with Tekke *gul*. 7'5" by 4'8".
Photo courtesy Perez (London) Ltd.

Right, a Bokhara prayer rug whose main field, divided by a wide cross bar and two
small upright *mihrabs*, is filled with dark candelabra-shaped figures.
Photo courtesy Sotheby & Co., London.

The Tekke prayer rug, called a *katchli* or *hatchlie*, is commonly known as a Princess Bokhara. The main red field is divided into four parts by a cross bar and two upright *mihrabs*. Bands of dark blue candelabra-shaped motifs fill the four quarters.

Pinde and Yomud Bokharas share the general characteristics of the Royal (Tekke) Bokhara, differing mainly in the exact configuration of the tribal *gul* and the shades of red used.

Beshir Bokharas have a greater variety of design than other Bokharas, showing a strong Persian influence in the floral patterns, including even the *herati*, and less rigidly geometric treatments. Typical Beshir colors are scarlet, light and dark blues, and yellows on a red ground.

The weave of Bokharas varies from moderate to fine; the Beshirs have 60 to 160 Persian knots per square inch, the Royal Bokharas range from 160 to over 300 Persian knots per square inch.

Design

Turkoman designs are angular and geometric in a limited color range. The primary design element is the *gul*, which appears in different configurations characteristic of individual tribes, such as the rose of the Salors, the flying eagle of the Tekkes. The polygonal *gul*—usually an octagon or diamond shape—is often quartered, with opposite quadrants using the same color scheme. The *guls* are arranged in rows across the field, with the intervening areas filled with geometric designs. Polygons, stars, crosses, and other geometric forms are complementary motifs. The side borders are often different from the end borders, but all contain related geometric shapes and motifs and are woven on the same color background as the field.

Color

The primary color of Turkoman rugs is red, ranging from dark purple or mahogany to bright

A Pinde Bokhara, identified by the distinctive *gul*, field motif, and borders, in brown, blue, and ivory on a dark red field. 3′3″ by 3′2″. *Photo courtesy Perez (London) Ltd.*

A Pinde gul

A Beshir whose narrow field is filled with a stylized *herati* motif borrowed from Persia. 14′ by 7′4″. *Photo courtesy Perez (London) Ltd.*

crimson and orange tones, used as the ground in both field and borders. The different shades of red are often associated with particular tribes. Motifs are woven in light and dark blue, white, yellow, browns.

Rugmaking Technique

Turkoman rugs are produced in both a flat kilim and a moderately dense pile usually tied with Persian knots, occasionally with the Turkish knot. The rugs are generally made of wool, with goat's hair sometimes used for the pile. The weave varies among Turkoman rugs, some have a short thin pile, others thick and long. The density of the weave also varies, from around 60 to over 300 knots per square inch.

To approximate the pile rugs use the Turkey tufting stitch on needlepoint canvas (*see* Chapter 17) or latch hooking (*see* Chapter 18).

To approximate the flat-woven kilims, use the Gobelin or Soumak stitch on needlepoint canvas (*see* Chapter 17).

Samarkand

In the geography of rugmaking, the natural bridge between Turkoman carpets and the rugs of China are the lovely weavings of Samarkand. Samarkand is actually a collecting place rather than a manufactory for rugs that are made in Kashgar, Khotan, and Yarkand in the far western Chinese province of Sinkiang.

Now part of Russia, Samarkand has had a long and turbulent history. The oldest city in Asia, and one of the oldest in the world, Samarkand has suffered at the hands of successive invaders, including Alexander the Great, the Arabs in the eighth century, and the Mongol hordes in the fourteenth century. Tamerlane brought to his fabled capital Chinese artists and craftsmen whose taste and skills were lasting. From his conquests of Bagdad and the Near East, he brought back Persian artisans.

The merging influences of China and Persia were important in producing the distinctive rugs marketed at Samarkand. From Persia came the flowers and rosettes, the tree of life, the vase pattern; from the Mongols, the religious symbols; and from China, the round medallions and fret borders, the peony, lotus, pomegranate, and cloud bands. The style is less angular than Turkoman rugs, not as graceful as Chinese.

57

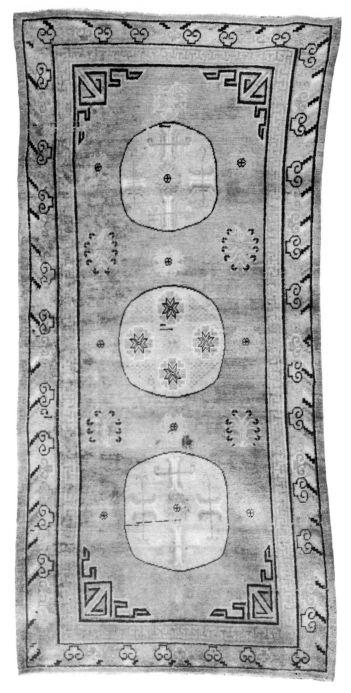

A characteristic Samarkand rug with three light blue medallions outlined in chocolate brown and laid out on a pale yellow ground. Four flower clusters growing out of urns flank the central medallion, and chrysanthemum rosettes are scattered over the field. The T pattern, cloud, and mountain borders are borrowed from the Chinese. 4' by 8'. *Photo courtesy Doris Leslie Blau.*

Design

Medallions in the shape of flattened circles are used in various configurations. One typical design has three medallions laid out on a field, colored in contrasting tones and surrounded by ornamental motifs like flowers, pomegranates, and trefoil leaves. Sometimes there is only one center medallion, sometimes portions of a medallion are woven into the corners. Another typical design is a pomegranate tree growing out of a vase. Sometimes the field is one color, sometimes there is an allover fret in a darker shade of the ground color, sometimes the ground is populated with Chinese figures of bats, butterflies, cranes, dragons, fish, and endless knots.

Samarkand borders are usually wider than those on Chinese rugs and often include a number of guard stripes. The main border may have a Chinese fret or T motif, a Chinese mountain or water pattern, the running swastika motif, or an angular vine.

Color

To the predominantly red palette of Turkoman rugs, the carpets of Samarkand have added mainly yellow; the colors are lighter, brighter, more mellow. Soft blues, gray, and tan are often used in the field; yellows, blues, and red in the design and border.

Rugmaking Technique

The pile rugs of Samarkand have a low density, usually 20 to 65 Persian knots per square inch. The rugs are generally made of wool, although a few, especially old Khotans, were woven with silk pile for the imperial palace in Peking—supposedly inspired by the Polish rugs of Persia.

To reproduce the texture, use the Turkey tufting stitch on needlepoint canvas (*see* Chapter 17) or latch hooking (*see* Chapter 18).

Samarkand with central medallion surrounded by stylized butterflies and by chrysanthemum rosettes and long-stemmed flowers emanating from vases. The border motifs—T pattern, cloud, and mountain symbols—show their Chinese influence. 7'1" by 4'7". *Photo courtesy Perez (London) Ltd.*

Detail of the Samarkand *saph,* or multiple prayer rug, illustrated in the color section. These two neighboring panels (the second and third from the left) show how the same design was treated differently by effective use of contrast as well as color. *Photo courtesy Perez (London) Ltd.*

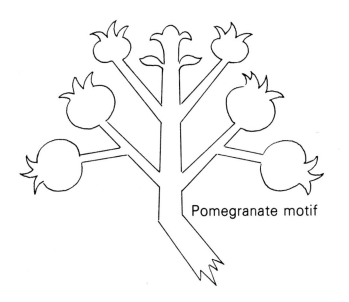

Pomegranate motif

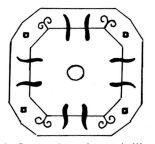

A Samarkand medallion

Chinese

Of all oriental rugs, Chinese carpets are among the most easily recognizable. The simplicity of design, the serenity of composition, the limited range of subdued and harmonious color, the symbolic motifs, and the borders all stamp their origins at a glance. Even compared with the closely related Samarkand weavings (actually made in the far western provinces of China), Chinese carpets are more refined and sophisticated, more subtle in their use of color, more imaginative in their choice of symbols and composition.

Contributing to this distinguishing style is the fact that Chinese rugs rarely have regional characteristics. Generally, Chinese carpets share the same symbols, patterns, and color schemes, except for rugs from Kansu and Suiyuan, which are closely related to each other in design and predominantly blue color scheme, and those designated as Ninghsia, a market place for rugs woven in that province or in Mongolia, which came to be applied indiscriminately as a term of quality.

The earliest surviving Chinese carpets date from the late Ming dynasty in the mid-seventeenth century, although rugs were probably woven well before then during the Sung dynasty (960–1279) when trade as well as literature and art flourished, and during the dazzling and luxurious Mongol court of Kublai Khan. After the Chinese reestablished their independence as the

Ming dynasty, their own artistic and cultural accomplishments, stimulated by the Mongols, were rejuvenated and reinvigorated. They completed the Forbidden City of Peking, with its temples, palaces, theaters, and courtyards. They printed dictionaries and other scholarly books. They produced the lovely and prized Ming porcelain.

The Ming era is as highly regarded for its rugs as for its porcelain. Carpet designs were simple arrangements of geometric forms. Typical was a round or octagonal medallion, sometimes incorporating a fretted or foliate dragon, on a plain field or against a subdued repeat pattern, often an allover fret. Narrow borders usually had one stripe, often a swastika fret, which eventually became a single line. The color scheme was as simple as the design; blues and browns predominated, with a soft yellow. The color of the border repeated that of the main field.

By the middle of the seventeenth century the Manchus seized power and overthrew the Mings. Their Ch'ing dynasty, and especially the reigns of K'ang Hsi and his grandson Ch'ien Lung, were splendid eras for the applied arts. K'ang Hsi, in an effort to invigorate native trade, asked painters to design for the weaving and carpet industries. The early K'ang Hsi designs were much the same as Ming. The forms, although becoming naturalistic, were still essentially geometric; foliate dragon motifs and fretted grounds were still popular. But there was a freer use of color and more ornamentation; scrolls, vases, and plants often covered the field.

Later K'ang Hsi rug designs were influenced by Manchurian taste and style, which were rejuvenating all the decorative arts. Graceful flowers, like the lotus and peony, replaced the geometric forms almost entirely, and even where central medallions and frets remained, flora and fauna were used in the field. Single color stripes were still popular for borders, but flower and vine forms supplemented the fretwork. Colors were brighter; the soft yellow, for example, now became imperial yellow.

Chinese weaving flourished in the last half of the eighteenth century during the long reign of Ch'ien Lung. The emperor loved carpets. He received them as tribute from neighboring Mongol tribes, he imported them, and he ordered them woven. Most of the old Chinese rugs in Peking palaces date from his reign. These are the most ornate and opulent Chinese weavings, incorporating Persian influences. Flowers, leaves, and buds are drawn with great accuracy and refinement, colors are shaded with subtlety and blend harmoniously.

These lovely rugs often have allover floral patterns, with compositions of flowering and budding chrysanthemums, narcissi, lotuses, sunflowers, orchids, and peach blossoms on the field. A butterfly may alight on a peony. A central floral medallion may be encircled by foliage, fruits, vases, fans, or Taoist symbols. Pearl, peony or T borders often framed the field. There was a wider use of color within a typical scheme of blue, apricot, cream, and white.

In the nineteenth century, Chinese rug weaving responded to the demands of the American and European markets. Obvious motifs from the past, like the dragon, were centered in the field and surrounded by a simple decorative border, perhaps a fret pattern or overlapping waves. Ornate floral designs derived from Aubusson patterns were also made, usually with a rich central medallion on a solid color field and edged by a heavily decorated border.

The aniline dyes introduced at the end of the nineteenth century and eagerly used in place of natural dyes profoundly transformed Chinese rugs. Colors which were once harmonious, related, and serene became harsh and garish. The large ungainly shapes newly borrowed from European design were represented in the unfamiliar purples, lilacs, and greens of the aniline dye vat. Even when the colors were toned down, the twentieth-century rugs were total departures from their oriental ancestors in coloring and often in design.

While most Chinese carpets were intended for

One of a pair of 19th-century pillar rugs laid flat. The blue-scaled imperial dragon contemplates a flaming pearl of perfection on a cloud-filled terra cotta field. The lower border displays the traditional mountain, cloud, and water symbols, the upper borders are shaded T and cloud band stripes. 3'8" by 6'3". *Photo courtesy Victoria and Albert Museum, Crown Copyright, London.*

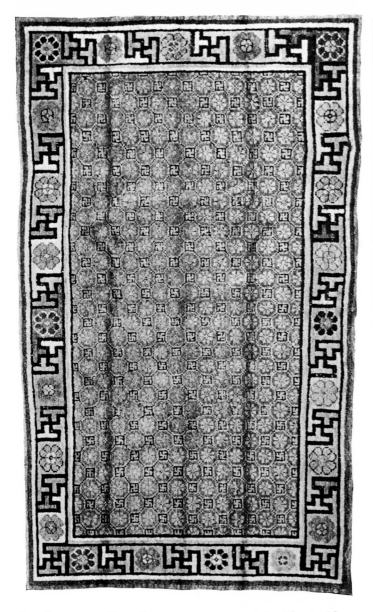

An allover swastika-and-rosette pattern contained by a wide border of alternating rosettes and swastika forms. 8′6″ by 5′6″. *Photo courtesy Sotheby & Co., London.*

use as floor coverings, from the late seventeenth century the Chinese have also woven their unique pillar rugs. Rather than lying flat on the floor, pillar rugs encircle the columns of palaces and temples during festivals. Tall and rectangular, they were usually made in pairs. A favorite design was a dragon or other figure whose coils stretched from one side of the rug to the other. When the rug is flat, the animal looks fragmented; when the rug is wrapped around a pillar, the coils are joined to complete the body. The lower border typically incorporates symbols of rocks and waves, the upper border often displays a variety of motifs.

Design

Chinese rug motifs predate rugmaking itself for they derive from silk weavings, which in turn come from ancient pottery designs. By the time of the Sung dynasty, more than fifty designs were identified by name, including the dragon and phoenix, the dragon medallion, lotus flowers, the lion (or Fo dog) with ball, floral symbol of long life, and characters representing happiness and good luck. These signs and symbols, among many others, are not exclusive to rugs but are also common to lacquer, jade, porcelain, and other applied arts. And because the Chinese so often cling to their ancient designs, many of them are still prominent in the rugs of today.

Geometric designs.   These are mostly of ancient origin. One or more are found on most carpets where they are used chiefly in borders and occasionally in fields. They include the dotted guard stripe called the pearl border; forms of the familiar Chinese border, also known as the meander, T, and key; dice and circle patterns in the field; and the various forms of the swastika or fret, the ancient symbol of good luck and most frequently used symbol in borders and fields.

Animals.   The   most   famous   animal,   of

Left, nine imperial dragons with long tails and whiskers chasing flaming pearls of perfection and surrounded by the traditional wave, cloud, mountain border. 12'1" by 9'4". *Photo courtesy Perez (London) Ltd.*

Right, nine Fo dogs amid cloud bands, surrounded by butterflies and cranes. The main border is a peony design, the inner stripe a pearl guard. 7'10" by 5'6". *Photo courtesy Perez (London) Ltd. and Sotheby & Co., London.*

Nineteenth-century silk rug with floral medallion and field designs, pearl guard stripe, and wide floral border. 7'10" by 5'. *Photo courtesy Perez (London) Ltd.*

course, is the dragon which, unlike western dragons, is beneficent. The four-clawed dragon keeps heaven from falling, the rivers on course, guards hidden treasures, and once every day six of them draw the chariot of the sun. The five-clawed dragon of the imperial court represents the emperor, and hence sovereignty or benevolent power. In designs the dragon is used singly or in pairs and sometimes in groups of five, seven, or nine. Occasionally it is associated with the phoenix, emblem of the Chinese empress, a marvelous bird with the head of a pheasant, beak of a swallow, tail and plumage of a peacock whose five colors symbolize the cardinal virtues.

Another popular animal design is the Fo dog, a Buddhist symbol resembling a lion. Defender of the laws and protector of Buddhist sacred buildings, the male is shown with a ball in his claw, the female with a litter of cubs. Other creatures occurring frequently in Chinese designs include the unicorn, stork, goose, the stag and crane for longevity, the elephant for strength and power, butterfly, and the bat, a frequently used symbol of happiness.

Flowers. Always realistic and identifiable, flowers are used in varied formations: in sprays, buds, blooms, in vases, and as an allover foliate design. The variety of bloom is large, each with its own symbolic meaning. Favorite flowers are the peony for wealth and status, the lotus for summer, the chrysanthemum for long life and autumn, the narcissus for winter and omen of year-round good fortune, the peach blossom for long life, the pomegranate for fertility, the plum blossom for beauty, orchid for fragrance, and the bamboo for longevity and enduring bloom.

Taoist symbols. These generally concern long life, and include eight important objects: sword, magic gourd, lotus, flute, bamboo clappers, basket of flowers, fan, and castanets.

Buddhist symbols. These include the eight emblems of happy augury: the flaming wheel of

Foliate central medallion whose design elements are repeated in the four corners. 6′ by 4′. *Photo courtesy Perez (London) Ltd.*

Lotus, representing summer

Chrysanthemum, symbol of autumn and long life

A peony medallion surrounded by flower sprays and an inner pearl guard, shaded T, and peony borders. 10'3" by 8'10". *Photo courtesy Perez (London) Ltd.*

the law, the state umbrella, conch shell, canopy, lotus, vase with the water of life, pair of fishes, and the endless or everlasting knot.

Natural forms. Reflections of the environment: clouds in puffs or bands used as central, corner, or border designs; a thunder line derived from the hieroglyphic for thunder; still water designated by tiered half circles and sea water by sharply angled tiers, used at the bottom of a scene or as a border; mountains often emerging from water; fire and lightning in flame-like scrolls.

Miscellaneous symbols. In addition to the myriad religious, philosophical, and natural forms, together with their symbolic meanings, there are other less easily categorized motifs that are important in Chinese rug design. From the Hundred Precious Things come vases, pitchers, tea kettles; a special group of Eight Precious Things: pearl, coin, rhombus, pair of books, paintings, the musical stone, pair of rhinoceros horn cups, and an artemisia leaf; and the Four Fine Arts of gentlemanly accomplishment, represented by a harp, chessboard, books, and paintings. There is a circle of happiness enclosing various Mongol designs; the *yin-yang* symbol, often surrounded by the eight trigrams of divination; the *shou* symbol of happiness in various forms; and the many variations of round medallions, at first simple in design, later filled with elaborate interior patterns. Curiously the wide range of motifs did not include any tribal or family insignias.

Chinese rugs are distinguished from other oriental carpets not only by the wealth of symbols and motifs, but also by their composition and arrangement. Whereas other orientals are arranged with balance and symmetry, often according to widely accepted principles of design, Chinese rugs are more imaginative and free. The Chinese rugmaker chose his motifs and objects arbitrarily and arranged them according to his fancy; bats flit singly, in pairs, even in groups over the field, puffs of clouds float around a medallion or line up more formally in borders; a selection of

A foliate medallion on a "grains of rice" field. The side borders display some of the Hundred Precious Things, the traditional end borders symbolize the mountains, clouds, and salt water with spray. *Photo courtesy Victoria and Albert Museum, Crown Copyright, London.*

Vase, one of the
Hundred Precious Things

Yin-yang symbol surrounded
by the eight trigrams of divination

Another treatment of the peony medallion and field design. Swastika frets fill the corners. 6'10" by 3'11". *Photo courtesy Perez (London) Ltd.*

One version of the Chinese symbol of happiness (shou)

Another version of the Chinese symbol of happiness (shou)

Precious Things proclaims the designer's interest in and respect for painting or poetry or chess. In fact, in a kind of design shorthand, some rugs can be classified by their symbols. The longevity rug displays the crane, stork, deer, and tortoise; the rug of happiness may group a bat, gourd, *shou*, and circle of happiness; books, pencils, brushes, and ink stands will mark the literary rug as the swastika, knot of destiny, swallow, and magpie designate a rug of good luck.

The symbols may be placed in seemingly random fashion on the field, grouped around a central medallion or motif, or, as in the case of the dragon and Fo dog, actually constitute the central motif. The background may be a solid color or an allover repeat design, perhaps a swastika fret, massed clouds, rows of circles, the "tiger skin" pattern of short black wavy lines on a yellow ground, or the "grains of rice" design in brown on a yellow field.

Borders were intended to frame and contain the interior design. The earliest borders were geometric—swastika frets, key and T forms—which evolved into scrolls and more ornate floral patterns, especially using the peony. Frequently used were a pearl (dotted) inner guard stripe, placed just outside the field, and a mountain and water border which sometimes incorporated clouds and sea spray.

Color

The coloring of Chinese rugs is quite unlike that of most other eastern carpets. Where Persian, Caucasian, and Turkish rugs generally use strong contrasting colors in great variety, Chinese colors are harmonious, related, often in graduated sequences and subdued tones, and frequently limited in the same rug to the shades of only one or two colors. This limited palette is comparable only to the various shades of red in Turkoman rugs.

The subtle and delicate coloring of Chinese rugs has attracted much interest, quite apart from the designs themselves, and scholars have

Flower medallions and floral forms in dark blue, ivory, and yellow on a yellow ground edged by T and peony borders. 8'9" by 5'7". *Photo courtesy Doris Leslie Blau.*

published lists of colors most frequently used. Here is a general consensus of color frequency listed in order of their popularity: royal or deep blue, yellow, light blue, apricot, ivory, dark brown, cream, old red, tan, green, persimmon, sapphire blue, peach, salmon, brownish red, brick red, greenish yellow, turquoise, copper, pink, and black.

In early rugs colors were often confined to soft yellow, blues, browns, and a warm fruit red. Later carpets widened the color range, still keeping the tones subdued, and three general color schemes emerged: an ivory ground with patterns in shades of blue; a yellow ground with patterns in ivory, white, blue, red, or another yellow; a red ground (persimmon, terra cotta, apricot, salmon, or strawberry) with motifs in blue, ivory, yellow, gray, and green.

Rugmaking Technique

Using weaving techniques very much like those of Persia, India, and Central Asia, Chinese rugs were made primarily of sheep's wool hand-knotted on vertical looms. Some rugs also had silk pile, and a lesser number used the hair of goats, camels, and yaks. The Persian knot was used for the field, the Turkish knot occasionally for borders. The pile was relatively long and the knotting coarse—30 to 60 knots per square inch—but the yarn was twisted so loosely that its ends opened and spread into tufts which gave a denser look to the surface. Toward the end of the nineteenth century, rugs for export were knotted more densely, with about 100 knots per square inch.

Designs were sometimes more clearly defined by clipping or incising the pile immediately surrounding a motif so that it stood out in relief. Sometimes the level of the entire field was sheared to create a raised pattern; sometimes the design was cut to make it lower than the field.

To approximate the weave of a Chinese carpet, use Turkey tufting on needlepoint canvas (*see* Chapter 17) or latch hooking (*see* Chapter 18).

From the West

The rugs of the West, particularly those from Europe, owe a great deal to the weaving of the East. Conquest, migrations, trade, and political involvements brought oriental rugs westward. The conquering Moors carried them to Spain and then to France; a royal British marriage with a Spanish princess introduced them to England; Venetian traders sold them to the English peerage; Persian shahs gave them to European nobles. And techniques as well as designs had their influence. Turkish and Persian knots were adopted in the Savonnerie pile carpets of France and Axminsters of England, and as a Spanish knot in Spain. And just as the East had its flat-woven kilims and Soumaks, there were the flat-woven Aubussons of France and the tapestry weaves of the Navajos.

But despite the eastern influences, the rugs of western countries flourished in more diverse cultures, often developing indigenous and distinctive designs and techniques. The ryas of Scandinavia, for instance, with their thick, extra-long pile, answered the needs of a cold northern climate. Early American hooked rugs came from the thrifty recycling of outworn homespun clothing.

Nor are there common designs in the West. Oriental styles, despite their diversity, display recurring motifs. *Botehs*, swastikas, and star forms appear in every kind of eastern weaving. There is no such commonality in western design.

73

Neither is there the continuity of pattern found in eastern rugs. The Turkoman carpets of today have the same *guls* they had in the past; nineteenth-century Chinese rugmakers often used the ancient motifs of their ancestors; Persian village rugs have been woven in their characteristic designs for centuries.

Western rugs, on the other hand, are constantly changing and developing. Contemporary ryas, largely designed by fine artists, bear scant resemblance to the folk ryas of old. Twentieth-century French textile design is no more like French weaving of two hundred years ago than Matisse is like Fragonard. These evolving styles are in part the response of fashion to the social, economic, and political changes that have taken place so rapidly in the western world during the last few hundred years, and in part a response to the devastating effect of the Industrial Revolution. Textile technology, which mechanized the looms and created new patterns and weaves, forced the surviving craftsmen to explore and develop new directions in hand weaving.

As a group the vast variety of western rugs is no more or less valuable than oriental rugs; appreciation of them is entirely a matter of taste. Just as oriental rugs have their passionate devotees, there are those who delight above all in the interplay of form and color of a Navajo eye-dazzler, in the charming naïveté of an Alpujarra peasant rug of Spain, or in the luminosity of a contemporary Finnish rya.

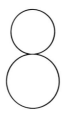

Spanish

In the world of rugs and carpets Spain is the gateway to Europe, bridging the weavings of East and West. Spaniards learned much from oriental rugmaking, adopting many aspects of technique and design, and developing and adding a characteristic style of their own. While other European countries were first introduced to the glories of rugmaking through the rugs themselves, which were traded or imported by visiting dignitaries and royalty, Spain learned the craft firsthand from the Moorish weavers and artisans who migrated to Spain from the northern shores of Africa early in the eighth century.

These Moors were recent converts to Islam and fanatic Moslems who, fighting in the name of Allah, crossed the Mediterranean and in 711 drove into northern Spain the Christian people who had been living in small isolated communities in the south. The Moors were often educated and wealthy, and they were accustomed to a civilized life which encompassed beautiful architecture and rich and luxurious furnishings. As they settled in southern Spain they brought with them not only their lovely household goods, but also the artisans and craftsmen who could duplicate in their new country the luxury they prized. Architects and engineers, gold and silversmiths, mosaicists, carvers, and weavers all settled in the fertile province of Andalusia and created a splendid world of palaces and furnishings, bridges and dams.

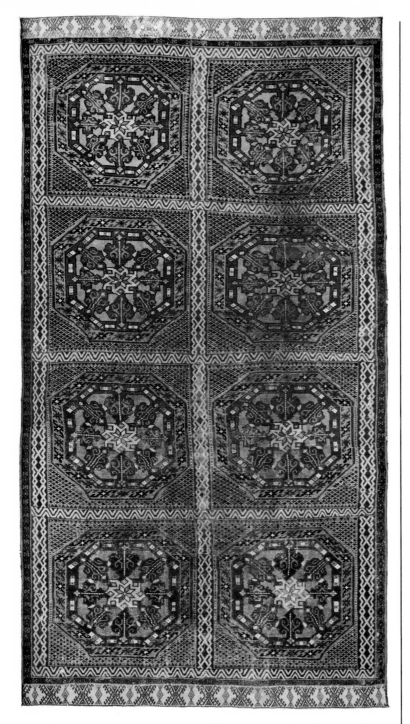

Hispano-Moresque rug in red, blue, green, and yellow, made about 1450 and incorporating rows of oriental-derived octagons with eight-point star centers. 10'2" by 5'6½". *Photo courtesy The Metropolitan Museum of Art, The Cloisters Collection, Purchase, 1953.*

The Moors soon dominated all Spain, first as artists and scholars, then for a time as rulers. They established Cordoba as the Islamic capital of Spain in 756, calling it the "Bride of Andalusia" for its beauty, which they believed rivaled Constantinople. The palaces of Cordoba were luxurious and extravagant, containing according to old records the richest and rarest carpets in the world. Cordoba itself soon became a center for study of poetry, art, law, and the sciences. By the ninth century the Moors had made Spain known throughout the world for its literature, engineering, architecture, and crafts, not the least of which was rugmaking.

The earliest Spanish carpets borrowed heavily from oriental designs and incorporated the geometric forms of Moslem art—six-and eight-pointed stars, triangles, circles, and borders with inscriptions praising Allah. Because the Islamic Koran forbade human or animal forms for decorative purposes, the designs were essentially geometric. The carpets were made of wool and used a limited palette of elementary colors—red, yellow, blue, and the two colors of good fortune, green and white.

The dazzling Moorish life style, especially in matters of taste and education, set a beguiling example for the Christians who had been driven north. Despite their deep religious differences Moors and Christians lived side by side, even as the Christians were slowly retaking their former cities and eroding the Moorish rule.

One of the more felicitous results of this curious coexistence was the emergence of a decorative style that combined Islamic and Christian motifs. Heraldic designs, for example, which began as simple coats of arms carried by the Crusaders, later combined with oriental forms and became an important early rug style. Sometimes called Admiral carpets because they were often woven for descendants of Spanish admirals, these long, narrow runners placed Western coats of arms and shields on a finely patterned field bordered by Kufic or Coptic script.

After Cordoba fell to the Christian kingdom of

An Admiral carpet of the 15th or 16th century with the coat of arms of Fadrique Enriquez, admiral of Castile, on a turquoise blue field patterned with a tan ogee trellis and floral forms. 6'2" by 4'11". *Photo courtesy The Metropolitan Museum of Art, Bequest of George Blumenthal, 1941.*

Two 16th-century Spanish rugs with characteristic motifs. *Left*, a pomegranate design in yellow on a blue ground. 8'3" by 4'5". *Photo courtesy The Metropolitan Museum of Art, Rogers Fund, 1913.*

Right, wreath design in green outlined in yellow on a red ground, winged dragon border. Full rug is 17'9" by 7'10". *Photo courtesy The Metropolitan Museum of Art, The James F. Ballard Collection; gift of James F. Ballard, 1922.*

Castile, Granada became the artistic and scientific center of Moorish life and the last stronghold of the Moors, surviving well into the fifteenth century. The Moors called it the "City of Dawn," and its great palace and citadel, the Alhambra, remains the finest example of Moorish architecture in Spain.

Granada also left its imprint on Spanish rugmaking. Many beautiful carpets were woven there, most dominated by its official color, red, and some incorporating the pomegranate, emblem of the city, which became an important motif in Spanish rugmaking. Some of the first carpets ever taken into England by Eleanor of Castile were from Granada.

Granada was still a great Moorish stronghold when Ferdinand of Aragon married Isabella of Castile, joining two fiercely Catholic houses. In the name of Christian unity, their joint armies drove the Moors from Granada in 1492, thus putting an end to Moorish rule in Spain, although not to the enduring influence of Moorish art and culture.

Perhaps in appreciation of their great cultural accomplishments Moorish artisans, carpet weavers among them, were allowed to settle in southern Spain. Some of them adopted Christianity and became *mudejars,* or converts, and all were closely supervised by the tyrannical Spanish Inquisition in what became known as the *mudejar* period. For over a hundred more years Moorish weavers worked in Spain under the watchful eyes of their Christian masters, and rug designs reflected this inhibiting influence. The typically Moorish octagon was abandoned and the laurel wreath and artichoke were introduced. Human and animal figures, which had been forbidden as decoration by the Islamic Koran, appeared. Alcaraz became an important weaving center, and later Cuenca, turning out fine and beautiful carpets often of baronial size for court and church use. But by 1609 Spain had driven out the last of the Moorish weavers and the craft of rugmaking, with all the other arts, started to decline.

After the Moors had been expelled from

Spanish star motif

Artichoke design

A Cuenca needlepoint carpet made about 1700 and displaying a stylized treatment of a wreath adorned with flowers and a border incorporating a pomegranate figure. 11'3" by 7'6". *Photo courtesy Kent-Costikyan, Inc., New York.*

Spain, trade with Christian France and Italy expanded, and the three countries shared many of their textile designs. The French fleur-de-lys was included in the Spanish coat of arms, and Italian Renaissance symbols like garlands, vases, and the acanthus leaf found their way into Spanish designs. After the eighteenth century, Spanish rugmaking virtually ceased, and the only rugs of any interest were being made by the peasants in the Alpujarra mountains of southern Spain.

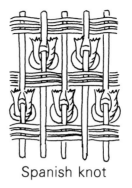

Spanish knot

Design

Moorish. Geometric oriental forms: six- and eight-pointed stars, octagons, triangles, circles, Seal of Solomon, Star of David; fields of geometric panels: diamonds, octagons, circles; Persian (Kufic) and Egyptian (Coptic) script as border or overall design in the field; borders of angular ribbonwork or leafy and floral vines; heraldic devices, including lion, castle; pomegranate.

Later Spanish. Wreath; artichoke; animals, including dragon, and phoenix, in borders.

Color

Spanish rugs used comparatively simple color schemes; often two colors predominate with a third for accent: blue and yellow, green and white, red and blue with a brown or ivory accent. Black and white, natural wool colors, were also used.

Rugmaking Technique

Hispano-Moresque rugs used a distinctive knot found in no other weaving. The Spanish knot is tied around one warp thread (rather than two warps as in Turkish and Persian knots) and around every other thread in alternate rows. This creates smooth diagonal lines instead of the smooth vertical lines produced by Turkish or Persian knots. Each row of Spanish knots is separated by one or three plain weft rows.

The Spanish knot was used in the Admiral carpets made at Letur and at Alcaraz. But when the carpet industry moved north to Cuenca during the seventeenth and eighteenth centuries, the Turkish knot was substituted. Sometimes the pile surrounding the design was clipped to create a bas-relief effect.

To approximate the texture of Spanish pile rugs, use Turkey tufting on needlepoint canvas (*see* Chapter 17) or latch hooking (*see* Chapter 18).

Alpujarra Rugs

Alpujarras are the peasant rugs of Spain, named for the Alpujarra mountain district south of Granada where they have been made for hundreds of years. They were probably first woven by Moors who took refuge in those verdant valleys after their expulsion from Granada at the end of the fifteenth century.

Alpujarra rugs are entirely different from Hispano-Moresque and *mudejar* carpets in every way. In design they are charmingly naïve and

Two Alpujarra rugs in the popular floral-vase-bird motif. *Left,* the design emphasizes the vase and flower against a dark ground. 7'8" by 6'3". *Photo courtesy Kent-Costikyan, Inc., New York.*

Right, a similar design in orange on an ivory field treating all three elements equally. It was originally made as a bed covering for the family of Antonio Mertines. 6' by 8'. *Photo courtesy Doris Leslie Blau.*

personal rather than elegant and sophisticated. Their geometric forms—squares, stars, circles, diamonds, rigid birds, and animals, flat flowers and trees—all characterize a primitive culture. There is little scale or proportion; animals are often larger than the trees. Sometimes a coat of arms appears, more often the name or initials of the person for whom the rug is woven. After the Catholic rulers finally drove the Moors out of Spain the Alpujarra peasants incorporated more Christian symbols into their rugs, like the cross, chalice, and sacred monogram.

In texture the peasant rugs are heavy and coarse, with thick low loops rather than the fine-cut pile of other Spanish carpets. They closely resemble early American hooked rugs. They are small in size because they were originally woven as bedspreads rather than as floor coverings; often two or three were joined for a rug.

Design

Geometric forms: stars, squares, circles, diamonds; tree of life, sometimes flanked by birds; vases, with and without flowers, sometimes flanked by birds; lions and other animals; pomegranates, the symbol of Granada, the province in which the Alpujarra district is located; borders of grapevines and leaves.

Color

Alpujarra rugs were woven in clear and vivid elementary colors: red, green, white, blue, yellow, and black. It was a simple color scheme in keeping with the simple designs. Rarely were all six colors used in one rug; more often just two appeared, sometimes with a third for accent. Some popular color combinations: blue and off-white, sometimes with red; red and black; red and green, sometimes with yellow; green and white; blue and yellow, sometimes with black.

Lion, often used as heraldic device

Example of a bird used in the Alpujarra peasant rugs

A vase as used in the Alpujarra peasant rugs

Rugmaking Technique

Alpujarra rugs are woven of coarsely spun wool on narrow looms in a technique quite different from that of other Spanish rugs. Here the weft thread is formed into loops over an iron rod, and the rod itself enmeshed and actually woven into the warp. The rod is then removed and wound with another row of loops. This process, which usually uses five or six iron rods at a time, forms a rough texture of raised loops, about 9 to 20 per square inch. Occasionally the loops are interspersed with sections of flat weave.

Another distinguishing feature of Alpujarras is their long fringe which oftened reaches eight or nine inches. It is woven separately, using one or more of the main colors of the design, then joined along all four edges of the rug. In contrast, the fringes of oriental rugs were made by knotting the ends of the warp threads at either end.

To approximate the texture of Alpujarra rugs, use the punch hooking technique (*see* Chapter 20).

French

Just as the history of France can be read through its decorative styles, the history of French rug-making is told by its most famous types of rugs —Aubusson and Savonnerie. Interrupted only by political crises and wars, the two manufactories have continued to make rugs for centuries, each using a different kind of weave.

Both types of rugs were made in the same prevailing fashion of design and differ primarily in their weave. Aubusson refers to the flat, or tapestry, weave of France; Savonnerie to its pile or tufted weave. The two terms describe only the weave of the fabric, not the place of manufacture, age of the rug, or period of design. In fact, both types of rugs came to be manufactured in many places in France and can be either old or new.

Aubusson weaving, the earlier of the two, began in the eighth century when the Moors invaded France, following their conquest of Spain. They were driven back by the armies of Charles Martel, but a few settled in south central France around Aubusson, a valley town on the Creuse river whose waters were especially effective in fixing the colors of dyes. Many of them built looms and became weavers, teaching the French natives the art. Their earliest weavings were tapestries in a small allover flower design resembling a *millefleurs* pattern. By the thirteenth century, French weaving had improved considerably,

Louis XV Aubusson carpet woven about 1770 for the chateau of the Marquis de Marigny, brother of Madame de Pompadour, displays sprigs of endive, reeds, and flowers in leaf green, royal blue, terra cotta, and rose on an oyster ground; the flowering vine border is on a brown field. 13′ by 17′. *Photo courtesy Perez (London) Ltd.*

and during the next two hundred years, the art of tapestry spread north and Paris became an important city in the weaving industry. By the sixteenth century, Aubusson tapestries were of a quality to proudly adorn the new chateaux built by a succession of French kings.

Francis I was the first to establish a dazzling court life. Extravagant in every way, he built many palaces, all of which required new furnishings, including tapestries for the walls and their heavier versions for the floor. He presided over the flowering of the French Renaissance, and his greatest legacies were the chateaux at Chambord and Blois in the Loire valley, and of Fontainebleau, where he established the French school of tapestry. His son, Henry II, expanded the weaving industry still further by establishing looms at Paris, Tours, and Felletin.

The wide use of tapestries and rugs in the newly built chateaux brought the French artisans in close touch with the crown and royal architects. But despite the demand for rugs and weavings, productivity sometimes rested on the religious serenity of the country. The weaving towns were centers of Protestantism, and the ranks of the Huguenots were swelled by Spanish Protestants fleeing the Inquisition in the late sixteenth century. During the Wars of Religion in the latter half of the century, weaving slowed and sometimes stopped altogether. The industry did not regain stability until Henry IV granted freedom of worship, through the Edict of Nantes, to the Protestants, among whom were many weavers and artisans.

Henry IV was raised a Huguenot, but he became a Catholic to heal the religious divisions of his country. A man of wit and moderation, he encouraged the development of new industries and expanded foreign trade. Happily for the rug industry, he was a great patron of weaving and established some looms in the Louvre for a young weaver named Pierre DuPont who claimed he could make pile carpets in the manner of oriental rugs. Perhaps to protect this young rugmaking factory and the new French pile rugs, or perhaps

Louis XVI Beauvais tapestry rug in wool and silk with garlands of flowers on a duck-egg blue ground. 5' by 3'8". *Photo courtesy Sotheby & Co., London.*

Aubusson in the style of Louis XVI. 11′8″ by 8′2″.
Photo courtesy Perez (London) Ltd.

Lion and cartouche

Shield with fleur-de-lys

Cornucopia with flowers

because the weaving centers of Aubusson and Felletin were among the first cities in France to acknowledge the former Huguenot as ruler, Henry banned the import of carpets from other countries, thus assuring the French rug industry of a prosperous market and climate in which French design could flourish.

The pile rug factory quickly outgrew its first quarters in the Louvre and moved into an abandoned soap factory, or *savonnerie*, then used as a children's home. Thus provided with a resident source of youthful labor to train in the craft of rugmaking, the factory produced Savonnerie carpets there for two hundred years until it moved its looms in 1825 to the *Manufacture Nationale des Gobelin*, a wool-dyeing and tapestry- weaving center in Paris that Henry IV had established as an official state factory to make the many wall hangings he needed for his chateaux.

From the first, production of Savonneries was controlled by the crown. Orders for royal rugs were so numerous and the carpets themselves so large that few but court carpets could be made. Louis XIV, for instance, ordered ninety carpets —some 16 by 30 feet—for Versailles; and the French Pope furnished his rooms at Fontaine-bleau with Savonneries.

The beginnings of a purely French style emerged with the reign of Louis XIV. This was a period of prosperity during which the king and his court built and furnished many palaces. The decorative style was called Baroque, massive and grand, large in scale and classic in proportion and balance. It was designed to glorify the king and through him the state. Furnishings were coordinated with architecture and landscape design, and the entire spectrum of court decoration was controlled by Charles LeBrun, the favorite court artist. Together with architect Le Vau and landscape architect Le Nôtre, they created Versailles, their masterpiece, which in twenty years was transformed from a small hunting lodge to a massive palace housing ten thousand people.

Huge court carpets were now a basic part of palace furnishings, and Le Brun created carpets

Louis XVI Aubusson rug ornamented with floral designs. The center medallion and inner floral border have pearl gray grounds, the main field is celadon, and the wide outer border is deep rose. 8'6" by 6'6". *Photo courtesy Kent-Costikyan, Inc., New York.*

Top, Empire Aubusson, about 1800, with floral medallion and corner bouquets on a brilliant emerald green field scattered with golden rosettes; red and blue flower border on a chocolate brown field. 9'6" by 8'.

Bottom, Louis Philippe Aubusson, about 1840, with floral bouquet in an ivory cartouche on a claret field; the ivory inner border is decorated with clusters of roses, the outer border is deep rose. 13'3" by 10'.

Both photos courtesy Kent-Costikyan, Inc., New York.

Opposite page, Directoire Aubusson, about 1830, showing the architectural influences of the style. Richly decorated in forest green, apricot, yellow, rust, and turquoise on a chocolate brown field. 11'6" by 14'. *Photo courtesy Doris Leslie Blau.*

for the Sun King's palaces. They were like classic French paintings, designed to harmonize with the décor and furnishings. Acanthus scrolls and the sunburst, the royal insignia, were popular. Motifs painted on the ceiling often appeared in the floor coverings so that, unlike oriental carpets which were at home in many kinds of décor, these French Baroque carpets could only be used in the room for which they were designed.

In the midst of this demand for great court carpets, Louis XIV dealt a heavy blow to the weaving arts when, under the influence of the devoutly Catholic Madame de Maintenon, he revoked the Edict of Nantes in 1685. Soon many looms fell idle as thousands of Protestant weavers and artisans fled the country.

The grand and imposing Baroque style of Louis XIV, who had ruled for seventy-two years, created a longing for a more personal and informal manner. The middle class developed a more modest style better suited to their country manors, and this was the origins of what we call French Provincial. Louis XV and the aristocracy, in their own reaction to Baroque opulence and splendor, created the graceful Rococo style of intimate luxury, universally pleasing in its softer tones and shapes. Large state rooms at the Louvre and Versailles were divided, requiring new and smaller scale rugs and furnishings. Asymmetrical curves replaced straight lines. Flowers, flourishes, and musical instruments superseded the trophies of war and emblems of state.

In the succeeding style of Louis XVI the romantic curves of Rococo gave way to a refined and fragile classicism of balance and delicacy. Fine scrolls, classic moldings, flowers, and acanthus leaves were used in restrained proportion. Gardening was in vogue, so bouquets, ribbons, even garden tools and large-brimmed sun hats appeared. Colors were pale and delicate.

While Savonnerie carpets went almost exclusively to the court and the royal family, the weavers at Aubusson made rugs for the general public as well. Aubussons were particularly well suited to

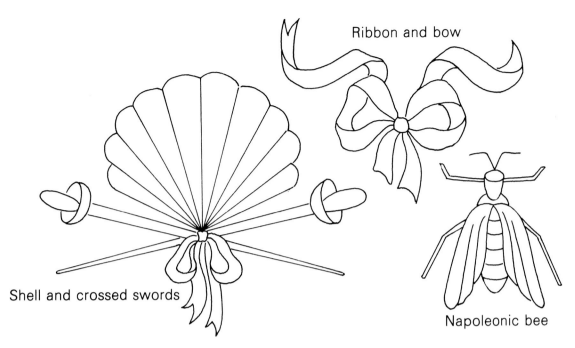

Ribbon and bow

Shell and crossed swords

Napoleonic bee

Large Empire Savonnerie carpet, pale green and pink on a pale yellow ground with brown and yellow borders. 17'9" by 13'2". *Photo courtesy Sotheby & Co., London.*

the public market place; the flat tapestry weave was quicker to work and required much less wool than the knotted pile, making production higher and price lower than Savonneries. The rug-buying public also found that the designs on the flat-woven Aubussons were clearer than on the pile Savonneries, and since the eighteenth century Aubussons have been fashionable.

The French Revolution put a stop to all the decorative arts. When rugmaking was revived under Napoleon, the Emperor, like Louis XIV before him, established state supervision over the arts. Turning to the design inspiration of ancient Greece and Rome, Napoleon tried to portray his imperial grandeur and battle triumphs with the symbols of war—swords, shields, helmets, flaming torches, and the imperial N entwined in victorious laurel wreaths. Soon after Napoleon was banished, the power looms of England dominated the European rug market, offering the middle class a wide variety of derivative styles, and by the end of the nineteenth century, the production of machine-made carpets all but eliminated hand weaving.

As one style often seems to breed its own reaction, the machine-made carpets provoked an anti-machine response. In France this resistance was called Art Nouveau, a style that emulated the Arts and Crafts movement of William Morris in England. This anti-machine school featured stylishly elongated flowers and twisting arabesque vines fashioned into sinuous designs. Inevitably, the elegant and romantic Art Nouveau also created its own reaction in Art Moderne, the French version of the Bauhaus, an international style favoring spare, severe, and functional forms in bold solid colors.

By far the most exciting revival of hand weaving and tapestry design in France began in the 1920s, particularly at Aubusson under the direction of the artist Jean Lurçat. Years later, when Lurçat was a Resistance fighter during World War II hiding out in Aubusson, the town weavers needed more designs for their looms. Lurçat drew a crowing cock standing on a blazing sun. The

Torch and arrows

Top, Jean Picart le Doux
Aubusson tapestry, "The
Net" (*Le Chalut*).

Bottom, Jean Lurçat's
cartoon for his tapestry,
"The Sky" (*Le Ciel*).

*Both photos courtesy
French Cultural Services,
New York.*

cock became a famous symbol of liberty, and the designs that he and fellow artists made for the Aubusson weavers energized a great and continuing renaissance in tapestry weaving that has attracted many fine painters to this medium, among them Miro, Dufy, Matisse, Gromaire, and Picard le Doux.

Design

Early Aubusson. Tiny flowers in an allover design.

Baroque. Large, well proportioned, and balanced designs with scrolls, acanthus leaves, rosettes, cornucopias, shells, cartouches, and the royal insignia, the sunburst. Simple borders with repeat acanthus motifs, crossed or twisted ribbons, cornered with fleurs-de-lys or acanthus leaves. The colors are rich and restrained; fields of blue, tan, black, green, red.

Rococo. Curved, asymmetrical lines; coquille shells, flowers, beribboned baskets of flowers, crossed arrows in the center or corners; romantic symbols like the lyre.

Louis XVI. Delicate classicism, with beribboned bouquets and garlands, urns of flowers, dainty rosettes, acanthus leaves, classic moldings and scrolls, Greek key, egg-and-dart borders. Light, delicate colors.

Empire. Heavy designs; N entwined in laurel leaf wreath, bumblebee, urns, sphinx heads, lions, cornucopia, garlands, drums, swords, large medallions, shields, helmets, flaming torches. Colors favored were brown, olive green, emerald green, royal blue, deep red, gold, black.

Art Nouveau. Elongated, romantic flowers, including the lily and tulip, and vines.

Art Moderne. Spare, geometric forms in bold elementary colors.

Jean Picart le Doux Aubusson tapestry. "The Open Cage" (*La cage ouverte*). 5'3" by 4'1". *Photo courtesy French Cultural Services, New York.*

Rugmaking Technique

Aubusson rugs and hangings are made in a flat tapestry weave; for durability, the rugs are heavier and coarser than the hangings. Both are woven on vertical or horizontal looms on which the warp threads run the width of the work (rather than the length as for pile rugs) so the project is actually woven from side to side. The design is formed as the weft threads are interwoven and tightly packed down to cover the warp. Aubussons have no fringes; the four sides are customarily hemmed.

To approximate the flat tapestry weave of Aubusson, use the Gobelin stitch on needlepoint canvas (*see* Chapter 17).

Savonnerie rugs are hand knotted on vertical looms. Starting at the bottom, a row of knots is tied across the warp threads of the loom, usually by looping them over a long metal rod with a cutting edge at one end. When the entire row of knots has been tied, the rod is removed and the blade cuts the weft loops into pile as it is pulled out. Several rows of plain weft threads may be interwoven between each row of knots.

To approximate the pile of a Savonnerie rug, use Turkey tufting on penelope needlepoint canvas (*see* Chapter 17) or latch hooking (*see* Chapter 18).

English

Although Britain came relatively late to the manufacture of rugs and carpets, her contribution was distinctive and far-reaching—first, in the delightful naturalistic floral designs that are typically English, and second, in the development of modern, mechanized methods of carpet production which profoundly affected the entire industry.

While France and Spain were enjoying the luxury of woven wall hangings and floor coverings, England knew practically nothing of pile carpets until Eleanor of Castile came to England in 1254 to marry Edward I and brought oriental and Spanish rugs with her. She furnished her rooms in Westminster with wall tapestries and rugs, partly for aesthetic reasons and partly to ward off the cold and damp. The luxurious display completely shocked the English, who customarily covered the royal floors with straw.

Hay and rushes remained the preferred floor covering for over two hundred more years, and it was not until the sixteenth century that we find much evidence of carpets. Turkish rugs appear in portraits by Hans Holbein the Younger, court painter of Henry VIII, whose work is an invaluable index of the furnishings of the period. The style of these Holbein rugs was so popular that the rugs themselves were imported, or later copied, delaying the emergence of any style more typically English.

Knotted pile embroidery
dated 1672 incorporating
a black and white coat of
arms on a densely strewn
field of bright flowers.
*Photo courtesy Victoria
and Albert Museum,
Crown Copyright,
London.*

During the early sixteenth century, the growth of the English merchant fleet and the accessibility of mideastern ports encouraged the importing of rugs. Cardinal Wolsey, Henry's powerful lord chancellor, managed to get sixty oriental rugs from Venice to adorn his lavish home, Hampton Court, and this started a vogue among the nobility for these rich and sumptuous furnishings. All of these orientals came to be called Turkey carpets because the earliest ones were woven in Turkey, and the rest were shipped from there.

The importation of oriental carpets was effectively stopped, however, by Spain and other Catholic countries which closed the Mediterranean ports to British ships when Henry VIII established the Church of England and divorced his Spanish wife, Catherine of Aragon. Not until 1588, when Sir Francis Drake defeated the Spanish Armada, were the sea routes to the East again opened.

During the period when eastern carpets were not available, an English weaving industry developed, encouraged by Cardinal Wolsey, to produce floor coverings for the nobility whose taste and appetite for this fairly recent luxury had been whetted. Labor was cheap and wool abundant, and for the first time an English rug style began to emerge, appropriately finding its roots in the gaily colored flowers of an English garden.

These sixteenth century hand-knotted rugs and embroideries were a mass of flowers and blooms, flowering in the same variety as an English garden—with roses, columbines, lilies, pinks, tulips, daisies, poppies, cornflowers, narcissi, and living creatures of the garden, including butterflies, caterpillars, insects, even worms. Queen Elizabeth's favorite flower, the purple and yellow pansy, was particularly favored, and her initials, ER, for Elizabeth Regina, were often incorporated in the border.

The bright floral designs actually derived from the hand embroidery of the country women which was called "Turkey work," referring to its long-pile embroidery stitch that resembled the hand-woven Turkish knot. It was made in bright

Needlework embroidery, about 1600, worked in the longarm cross stitch with 13 stitches to the inch. The Turkish influence is evident in the light and dark octagons with interior geometric tracing and the blue Kufic type border. Roses and pansies fill the light green diamonds. *Photo courtesy Victoria and Albert Museum, Crown Copyright, London.*

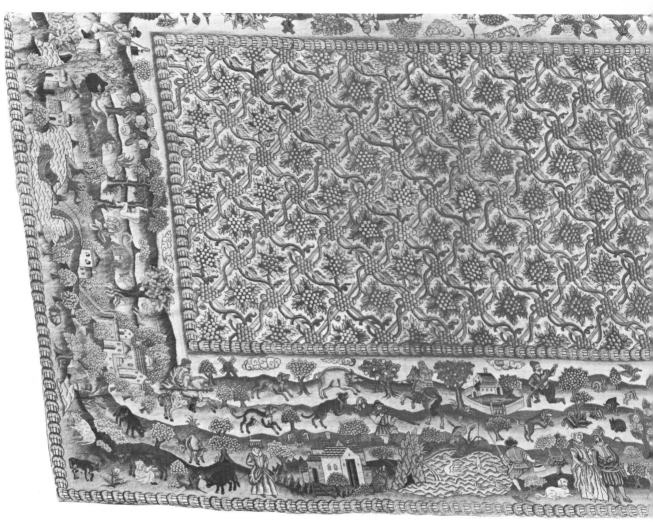

Elizabethan table carpet, about 1600, worked in silk on linen in the tent stitch which pulled the embroidery askew. A wide pictorial border of detailed scenes of country life surrounds the latticed floral field. *Photo courtesy Victoria and Albert Museum, Crown Copyright, London.*

Swag with bow, fruit and flowers

reds, blues, and greens, in small pieces to be thrown over chests, tables, stools, chairs, and beds as upholstery fabric in the fashion of the day.

When the trade routes to the Mediterranean were reopened toward the end of the sixteenth century, oriental rugs were again imported. The growing English rug industry turned once more to copying eastern designs, even as it continued to produce its own indigenous floral patterns. At the same time it sought to improve its techniques and meet a growing demand for lower priced floor coverings by adapting existing broadcloth looms to rug production.

Ironically the struggling young industry was invigorated by the same political act that dealt a heavy blow to French rug weaving—the revocation of the Edict of Nantes in 1685. When Louis XIV revoked the edict which had protected the rights of French Protestants, he drove sixty thousand Huguenots to England in search of religious asylum. Many of them were weavers who naturally settled in the established weaving centers and brought with them their ideas and skilled techniques. By the end of the century, the burgeoning industry asked King William III for protection against unskilled competition and received a charter permitting a trade association that could issue certificates after seven-year apprenticeships, thus cleansing the expanding industry of shabby artisans.

In the eighteenth century fine carpets were produced at many weaving centers for an eager market. For many of its inhabitants, rapidly growing Georgian London was an elegant city. Town houses were now part of the urban scheme, and they needed furnishing. A large leisure class turned its attention to the arts, not least of which was home decoration. To aid them, the Society of the Dilettanti was formed and it had great influence on architecture and the decorative arts. The Royal Society of Arts offered an annual competition for carpet design, with Thomas Moore and Thomas Whitty, later two of Britain's leading rugmakers, sharing the first award.

Large and elegant carpet of the mid 18th century. The two peacocks stand proudly amid a profusion of flowers, corner baskets of flowers, and a family of ducks at center top and bottom. 21'4" by 15'10". *Photo courtesy Sotheby & Co., London.*

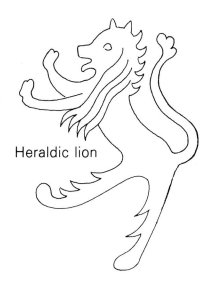

Heraldic lion

A late 18th-century Axminster in a classical arrangement of medallions, garlands, and bouquets made for the Brighton Pavilion. *Photo courtesy Victoria and Albert Museum, Crown Copyright, London.*

Whitty had just established a small carpet works at Axminster and was determined to duplicate an oriental rug he had admired at the home of a friend. After an unsuccessful try at weaving one on his own horizontal fabric loom, he studied the upright loom of Peter Parisot who had worked at the Savonnerie. Then he returned to Axminster and built a large vertical loom and started weaving in the oriental manner, using Turkish knots. Whitty produced good work at low prices and his shop flourished, run by his descendants until 1835 when it merged with the Wilton factory. Today Axminsters are made at Wilton by machine and until recently by hand. Although no rugs have actually been made at Axminster for well over a century, the name survives and refers to English pile carpets in much the same way that Savonnerie refers to French pile rugs.

Shortly after Whitty started making knotted carpets at Axminster, Claude Passavant, a wool merchant, set up a rug center at Exeter and soon bought out the equipment of his fellow Frenchman, Parisot. Not much later Thomas Moore established his own workshop for hand-knotted rugs at Moorfields, in London.

These three leading rugmakers reflected the decorative taste of the eighteenth century. Classical designs of Greek and Roman derivation were popular, as were motifs from oriental carpets. Thomas Whitty's designs were classical arrangements of medallions, beribboned bouquets and garlands. Passavant's were more rococo, with scrolls, flowers, and leafy motifs. Thomas Moore epitomized the neoclassical style of Robert Adam, the famous architect and designer who dominated the decorative taste of England at the end of the eighteenth century and influenced every kind of interior furnishings, from plaster walls and ceilings to furniture, rugs, and silver. Moore worked closely with Adam, adapting his refined classicism to carpet design with swags, wreaths, urns, medallions, rosettes, frets, honeysuckle motifs, Greek keys. It was an elegant style

Knotted pile rug made at Exeter in 1757 by Claude Passavant in a rococo design of birds and tables laden with flowers and fruit surrounding a dog on a cushion, all framed by leafy scrolls. *Photo courtesy Victoria and Albert Museum, Crown Copyright, London.*

Top, a Robert Adam design for Osterley Park House executed by Thomas Moore in a knotted pile carpet.

Bottom, a carpet handmade at Wilton about 1837. 29'3" by 17'3".

Both photos courtesy Victoria and Albert Museum, Crown Copyright, London.

very much like the contemporaneous French Louis XVI period.

In addition to the recognized tastemakers of the eighteenth century, English needlewomen continued to influence design. Needlepoint rugs, long a diversion of the leisure class, became particularly popular in the eighteenth century when hand knotting of carpets began to decline. These needlepoint rugs, made primarily in the tent or cross stitch, were usually fairly large—6 to 7 feet wide and 9, 10, 11, even 12 feet long. Their design was still the ever-popular profusion of naturalistic flowers and leaves.

While many of the weaving centers continued to produce fine hand-knotted and tapestry-weave rugs for the rich, some factories were making carpets at less cost for the middle class. The beginnings of a mechanized carpet industry had already begun when Brussels looms were set up at Wilton in 1740. These looms produced excellent loop carpet that was woven in continuous rolls about 27 inches wide. It was first made in Belgium using a technique so closely guarded that, according to one apocryphal tale, the first weaver who brought the method to England had to be smuggled out of Flanders in a sugar cask. Eventually a cutting process was added so the loops could be sheared into a velvet-like pile still made at Wilton.

The great industrial advances of the eighteenth century inevitably had a profound effect on the carpet weaving industry. Arkwright's improvements of the spinning jenny in 1769, produced uniform yarns quickly and at low cost. Watt's patent on the steam engine in the same year, coupled with electricity, led to the power loom twenty years later. Jacquard looms, developed in 1800 by the Frenchman Joseph Marie Jacquard, revolutionized carpetmaking as well as every other material that incorporated a woven pattern.

Scotland, too, contributed to the British carpet industry. A flat, multiple cloth weave called ingrain carpeting was made in such quantity that it was often called Scotch carpeting. It produced a

Redcar, a late 19th-century hand knotted rug designed and made by William Morris with stylized flowers and leaf border. 11′ by 8′2″. *Photo courtesy Victoria and Albert Museum, Crown Copyright, London.*

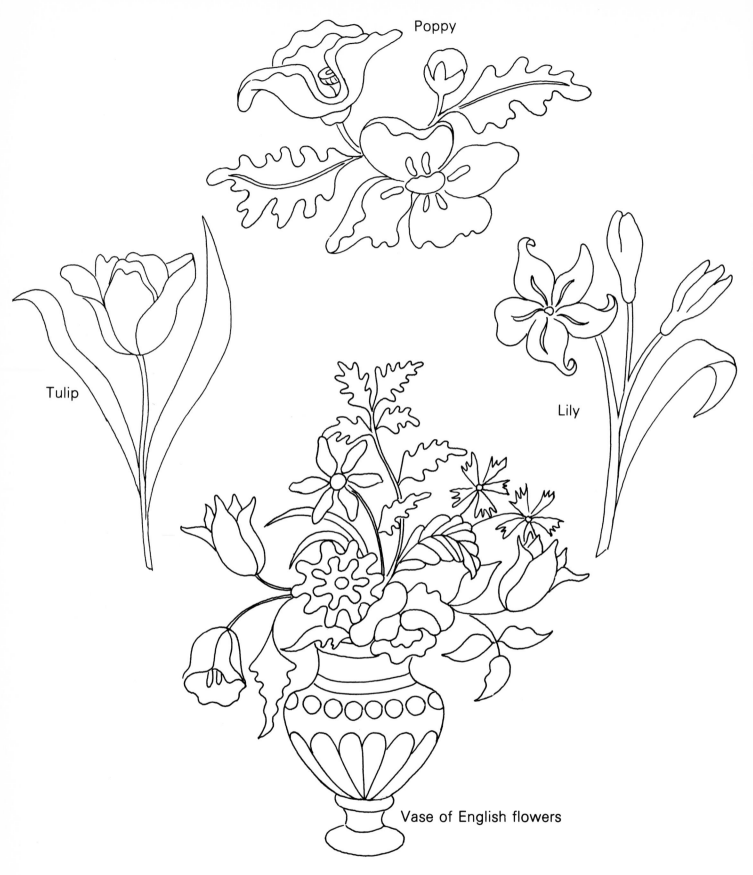

Poppy

Tulip

Lily

Vase of English flowers

pileless rug of double construction, with yarns from two parallel cloths interwoven with each other, and the design reversed on the back, much like damask. Machine-made chenille and tapestry weave carpets also originated in Scotland in the 1830s.

The industrialization of the nineteenth century blew the factory whistle on hand-knotted carpets. Power-driven looms were turning out carpeting by the yard in such quantity that they virtually drove out the higher priced hand-knotted rugs. With machine goods available at low cost and priced for every budget, most homes in England were carpeted against the damp and often chilly climate. The looms at Wilton, Kidderminster, and other centers were humming with activity, hard pressed to keep up with demand.

Power looms affected carpet design as well as production. Initially rug styles were more restrained, perhaps because of the limitations of the new looms. With technical refinements, manufacturers could produce more intricately designed rugs, and by the end of the century the machines could weave an immense variety of carpets.

Whether made by hand or machine, carpet designs followed the prevailing decorative fashions. The refined classicism of Robert Adam and the Georgian period was followed by the English Regency, which closely paralleled the French Empire style of Napoleon. There was a revival of oriental motifs; in furniture, the popular cabinetmaker Thomas Chippendale developed his own *chinois* style. Carpets and rugs carried out the Chinese vogue, with serpents, dragons, and the sacred symbols.

With the Victorian age pattern sprouted everywhere. Rooms were paneled in and furniture was made of dark woods such as black walnut, mahogany, ebony and rosewood. The wood was covered with ornately carved design elements such as fruits, flowers, bouquets, and leaves. The dark colors of carpeting and embroidery—maroon, green, black—duplicated the effect of the dark woods.

While most of middle class England was enjoying the fruits of the power loom, a few artists revolted against the machine technology and the bad taste of the Victorian age and tried to improve the quality of home furnishings. Led by the designer William Morris, the group spearheaded the Arts and Crafts movement that emphasized nature, handcrafts, and original design in the decorative arts. Morris himself studied all aspects of hand crafts. He learned to dye and to weave. His designs influenced the Art Nouveau period in Europe, using naturalistic flower forms in an attenuated, fluid style, often bordered with a wide strip containing leaves on a wavy stem. But perhaps his most lasting contribution to the decorative arts was the school he persuaded the government to set up to train artists in industrial design. And under his enthusiastic prodding, there was a revival of hand-knotted rugs and hand-woven tapestries.

Design

Flowers are the great English contribution to design. All kinds of flowers appear in English rugs and carpets: roses, columbines, lilies, pinks, pansies, tulips, daisies, poppies, cornflowers, narcissi.

Tudor. Intricate arabesques, vines, and stems were incorporated, as well as butterflies, caterpillars, worms, insects. Initials, dates, coats of arms and other emblems were occasionally included.

William and Mary. Plain or lattice ground with floral medallions and floral borders. Flowers, massed or in sprays, were sometimes strewn on the field. Coats of arms and dates still appeared.

Queen Anne. Small repeat lattice design over the center field framing a floral medallion; floral borders.

Georgian. Neoclassical revival and influence of the Adam brothers; swags, wreaths, urns, me-

A needlepoint rug stitched by H. M. Queen Mary, 1941–46, and auctioned for war charity. Each of the 12 panels has a different floral arrangement. *Photo courtesy The National Gallery of Canada, Ottawa, and presented by H. R. H. The Princess Elizabeth on behalf of the Imperial Order Daughters of the Empire, 1950.*

dallions, rosettes, frets, honeysuckle motifs, Greek key; a Pompeiian influence, with large central architectural forms enclosing floral motifs and flanked by elongated diamonds. A soft green was so popular it was called Adam green.

Regency. Revival of oriental motifs, including serpents, dragons, Chinese symbols.

Victorian. Fruits, flowers, bouquets, leaves; maroon or wine, dark green, black.

Art Nouveau. Naturalistic flowers in elongated forms; creamy pastel colors.

Color

Green is used liberally in all English rugs, both in the pattern and on the field. Other popular ground colors are dark brown and black to set off the vivid floral designs. Flowers were often shaded in tones of white, ivory, gold, pale blush to crimson, blue greens.

Rugmaking Technique

English pile carpets were woven very much like oriental rugs, always using the Turkish knot. The warp threads were strung to the desired width between two timber rollers, then rows of knots tied and secured with weft rows. As the work progressed from bottom to top, the finished carpet was rolled around the lower beam while additional lengths of warp threads were unrolled from the upper one.

To approximate the pile weave, use Turkey tufting on penelope needlepoint canvas (*see* Chapter 17) or latch hooking (*see* Chapter 18).

Needlework rugs were usually made in the tent or cross stitch, both of which are still popular today. For rugmaking, the tent stitch is most successfully made by the basketweave method (actually the diagonal tent stitch). For both needlepoint stitches, *see* Chapter 17.

11

Scandinavian

The geographic isolation and severity of life in the northern countries produced the unique kind of weaving we know as rya, which means, shaggy pile. The harsh climate made warm coverings a necessity, and the long hours of darkness encouraged the development of weaving and other indoor crafts. Almost every home had at least one loom and the women used the long winters to weave rya coverings to ward off the cold: bedspreads, seat covers, carriage and sleigh robes, hangings, and eventually rugs. Their ryas were family treasures handed down from one generation to the next.

The technique of weaving pile fabrics was known in Scandinavia as early as the Bronze Age, but the fashion of wearing tufted clothing began much later with the Vikings. By the Middle Ages, rya weaving and its uses had spread to the coasts of all the Scandinavian countries touched by Viking culture.

The most important article of Viking clothing was the tufted cloak. It was large and usually red, a color the Vikings loved. At night it was used as a cover or sleeping rug and as protection against the cold and damp on long sea voyages in open boats. When a Viking chieftain died, he was laid to rest on his rya cloak, and sometimes even wrapped in it.

Because most of the ryas from the Viking era were made for seafarers, they were called boat

UBI·NUNTII·

A scene from the Bayeux Tapestry showing the Duke of Normandy clad in a red and white costume woven by the rya technique. *Photo courtesy Finnish Society of Crafts and Design, Helsinki.*

ryas in Norway and island ryas in Finland. One rya was spread on the bottom of the boat, pile up, for a soft mattress, and a second laid tufts down for the blanket—the sailor sleeping between the two soft pile surfaces. They were woven from the water-resistant wool of their home-bred sheep in the natural colors. The thick yarn was knotted tightly and the pile was long, about two or three inches. Because the early looms were narrow, sometimes two or more ryas were joined together so that several sailors could share them.

These boat ryas had little decoration; dyes were expensive and probably not able to withstand the salt sea water. But sometimes a stripe of solid color or checks was woven around the rya, and occasionally the owner's mark was added for identification. One diamond pattern was common and by about 1,000 A.D. it had spread with the Vikings to all the coasts of Scandinavia, from Norway to Finland, Estonia, and East Prussia. It survived, in practically the same diamond form, to the end of the nineteenth century.

Eventually ryas began to be used as bed covers in homes as well as on boats, replacing animal pelts and fleeces. The long pile underside was usually left the natural color of the wool—white, gray, or brown—but more decoration, often bands of color, was added to the smooth side that showed. Shades of yellow, brown, and green were introduced, made from Finnish plant dyes; but reds and blues, which had to be imported from Germany, were used sparingly because of their high cost.

During the sixteenth century the weaving and exporting of ryas came under the protective eye of King Gustavus I of Sweden, who encouraged the development of national industries and the expansion of foreign trade. During his reign in the first half of the sixteenth century, ryas were woven in the castles of Finland and the craft spread to the nearby regions. In Sweden, Norway, and Denmark, wealthy families imported fabrics from southern Europe; but in Finland gentlewomen regarded weaving and handwork as a proper and creative pastime for well-educated

Red, white, and black boat rya in the popular diamond pattern. *Photo courtesy Finnish Society of Crafts and Design, Helsinki.*

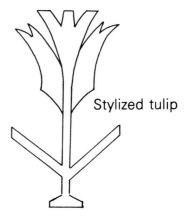

Tree of life motif

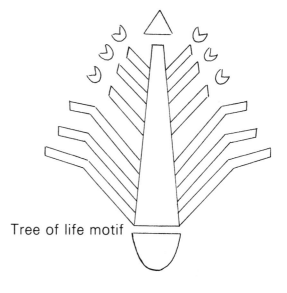

Stylized tulip

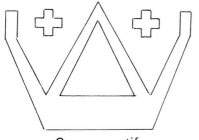

Crown motif

Heart motif

Ecclesiastical motifs appear frequently in rya designs. *Top,* a 16th-century diamond pattern with crosses edged with an ancient sawtooth border; in red, white, and black.

Bottom, a rya using letters from the church hymn board.

Both photos courtesy Finnish Society of Crafts and Design, Helsinki.

young women. It is generally believed that the most beautiful ryas come from Finland, particularly from the south and west, and indeed, the Finnish weavings were so lovely that one Swedish duke took some with him when he went to court Queen Elizabeth of England on behalf of his brother.

These sixteenth-century designs were primarily geometric: a checkerboard design, diamond motifs in white, dark brown, yellow, and blue, a large simple cross, probably derived from the medieval bier cloth which was laid over a coffin during burial. A multiple cross rya known as a bishop's rya was often used in church for the pastor to stand on during the church service to ward off evil spirits as well as a chill.

Inspired by the example of the bishop's rya, bridal couples also placed ryas under their feet during the church wedding service. After the ceremony this floor rya would be used as a cover for the bridal bed, so the shape and size changed to fit the normal bed. The growing popularity of the bridal rya had the young girls weaving them for their marriage chests incorporating all kinds of romantic motifs—hearts, the tree of life, initials, a representation of the wedding couple, and most usually the year of the nuptials.

Because the bridal rya was spread pile up on the floor of the church and pile down on the bridal bed, both sides of the rya—the tufted and the smooth—had to be beautiful. The solution was to knot tufts on the smooth side as well, at first only around the edges, then gradually over the entire surface. This shorter pile of finer threads on the smooth side became more and more decorative, while the long tufts on the underside remained in natural wool colors. By now, the ryas were actually double tufted, heavy, and exceptionally warm as well as decorative.

As the upper side of the rya became more heavily decorated, the rya itself increased in value and transcended its purely utilitarian function in the household. Designs became extraordinarily beautiful, and the once-humble bedcover was now reserved only for very special occasions—

Bridal ryas commonly incorporate a tree of life and stylized forms representing the bridal couple, wedding guests, animals, and houses, and occasionally the year of the nuptials. *Photo at left courtesy Galerie Hörhammer, Helsinki; at right, courtesy Finnish Society of Crafts and Design, Helsinki.*

"Once Upon a Time,"
designed by Mirja Tissari
in 1966. A contemporary
composition in black and
white reminiscent in its
circular movement of the
early wheel pattern.
*Photo courtesy Friends
of Finnish Handicraft
and Finnish Society of
Crafts and Design,
Helsinki.*

weddings, major festivals, and for the pleasure of important guests. As it became more and more an ornamental textile, the warmth of the rya no longer mattered and the extra-long shaggy pile on the underside disappeared altogether.

Folk rya weaving declined in the nineteenth century, partly because of foreign stylistic influences and partly because of the cheap aniline dyes that came onto the market and affected weaving and handcrafts the world over. When rya began to flourish again at the turn of the century, it was no longer a folk art but an expression of the best artists in the Scandinavian countries.

The pioneer of modern Finnish rya was the painter Akseli Gallen-Kallela, who worked in the Jugend style which featured asymmetrical compositions, often with wave and fire motifs. The next artistic surge in design was in the 1920s and was dominated by Impi Sotavalta who designed symmetrical compositions of geometrically styled plant and animal motifs. Ryas were now hung on walls exclusively, so the knotted rows were tied at fairly wide intervals and the loops cut in straight lines. One color was used for each knot, resulting in a cold formal look that echoed the functional Bauhaus style on the continent.

More delicately shaded ryas appeared in the 1930s as artists sought to recreate the softness and richness of color that characterized the early folk ryas. The most notable designer of this period was Eva Brummer who began to experiment with new designs and weaving techniques. Instead of the former precise patterns, she made water-color sketches for her designs; the rya did not reach its final form until it was actually knotted on the loom. Moreover, instead of tying the same color into each knot, she combined different shades of color in one knot and cut their ends to varying lengths, creating soft, imprecise forms. Her themes derived from old Finnish ryas, and often included hourglasses, crosses, and simple geometric shapes transformed by her very personal, subjective technique.

Contemporary ryas are also a product of con-

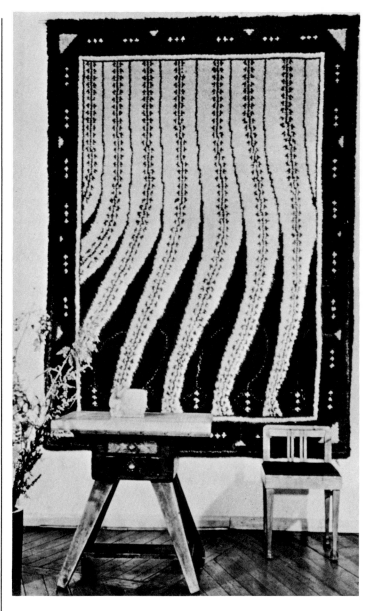

"Flame," designed in the Jugend style by Akseli Gallen-Kallela, father of modern Finnish rya, for the 1900 Paris World's Fair. *Photo courtesy Finnish Society of Crafts and Design, Helsinki.*

temporary artistic activity, and many leading Scandinavian artists are bringing their creative powers to this medium. Some of them look to the traditional folk ryas for inspiration and imbue them with new and subtle configurations and color; others explore totally new shapes and styles, from poetic motifs to Neo-Cubist forms.

Design

Early ryas were simple, woven in the natural wool colors of white, black, and gray, with occasional touches of natural yellow and red dyes.

As patterns became more sophisticated, leaves, circles, and rectangles of color appeared on the field, varying in size on the same rug. The composition was basically geometric, laid out along a central axis with the upper section different from the lower section. The year and initials were usually placed in the upper portion.

Ecclesiastical motifs inspired by church decoration and religious texts influenced design—the church window with its latticed glass design, the letters on the hymn board, and most of all, the cross, an important motif from early days.

The star motif, reminiscent of the eight-pointed oriental star, and a wheel pattern figured in designs, as did the tree of life.

Hannunvakuuna, the coat of arms of Hans and the traditional Finnish symbol from the epic *Karevala,* appeared in much Finnish folk art as a symbol of good luck. It was a square with circular corners. Coats of arms of ducal families were used in the middle of the sixteenth century.

In the eighteenth century figures of people in crude representations were used, as were hearts and palmettes, a Middle Eastern motif. Familiar objects of daily life—domestic animals, pets, people—were often included, and flowers in abundance, especially the tulip and rose. European motifs like wreaths, crowns, vases, and the heraldic lion traveled north to Finland via Sweden and its cosmopolitan court taste.

Color

In early ryas wool in its natural colors predominated, white, black, gray, and brown. Later, red, blue, green, and yellow were added. Contemporary ryas use a full range of color.

Rugmaking Technique

Ryas were woven on both horizontal and vertical looms of narrow width, so two or more ryas were often joined to produce a larger piece. Within the general category of ryas, there was a variety of weaves which included a flat tapestry and a woven Jacquard as well as the well-known long pile. The rows of pile were well spaced, often separated by 10 to 20 weft rows. The rya knot is actually tied like the Turkish knot, but the pile is much longer and the rows spaced much farther apart than in oriental pile rugs.

To approximate rya, use prewoven rya backing and the rya knot (*see* Chapter 19).

American Indian

The dazzling simplicity of Navajo blankets, the repetition of a few basic geometric shapes, and the artful yet minimal grouping of design elements have found a natural and responsive audience in contemporary collectors who sense in this nineteenth-century folk art a close affinity to the antecedents of abstract art.

The origins of Navajo weaving are far from purely aesthetic. The early Navajos were a nomadic tribe who settled principally in northwestern New Mexico. Their distinctive art forms of weaving and sand painting, their ceremonial rituals, and their newly agricultural life style were heavily influenced by the Pueblo Indians who had preceded them in the Southwest. With the coming of the Spanish, agriculture and herding became more important, and the Navajos began to settle in small communities. They tended large flocks of sheep, augmenting their numbers by periodic raids on their Spanish and Indian neighbors in the Rio Grande Valley from whom they stole livestock, food, and even women.

After the Pueblo Rebellion against the Spaniards in 1680, many Pueblo villagers sought refuge with the Navajos against Spanish reprisals, and it is likely that during this period the Pueblos taught the Navajos to spin and weave the wool of their sheep, using a primtive upright Pueblo loom that could easily be dismantled and transported. It was well suited to the seminomadic Navajos,

Serape style blanket, 1840–60, with its two basic elements—diamonds and stripes—in a superb composition using dark blue, red, and white. 5'8½" by 4'2". *Photo courtesy Los Angeles County Museum of Art and Southwest Museum, Los Angeles.*

and bore a striking resemblance to the simple vertical looms devised by the nomadic tribes of the Orient.

During the late eighteenth century the Navajo women perfected the art of weaving taught them by the Pueblo men and developed their own distinctive woven art form. Soon they were the major suppliers of native woven textiles in the Southwest, producing blankets which the Navajos wore, slept under, and hung over the doors of their homes for protection and decoration, but never used as rugs. Primarily, Navajo blankets were a very personal article of clothing worn by men, women, and children. They were woven in designs and sizes to please the individual wearer; men's blankets were generally about 50 by 70 inches, women's about 45 by 60 inches, and children's about 35 by 59 inches.

By the middle of the nineteenth century the Navajos had reached a period of great technical achievement in spinning and weaving. They used hand-spun yarn primarily in the natural colors of their sheep's wool—white, black, and brown— and augmented this with Saxony yarn from Germany and a limited palette of dyed colors, primarily blue and red. The blue came from an indigo dye they got from the Spanish, and the red from *bayeta*, the Spanish name for baize, the English flannel cloth. *Bayeta* came in many colors but the Indians preferred red above all. They carefully unraveled the woven bolts to retrieve single strands which they then used in twos, threes, or fours, twisted together or not, as weft threads.

Early Navajo designs were simple, usually stripes woven in colors of random widths. Later, rectangles, crosses, zigzag horizontal lines, and diamond shapes were added, all at right angles to the warp so that diagonal lines were formed in steps or terraces. Sometimes the diamond pattern was laid out on a solid red ground, sometimes on a striped field; it came to be known as *bayeta* serape style because of the liberal use of the favored red color.

Another important design of this great classi-

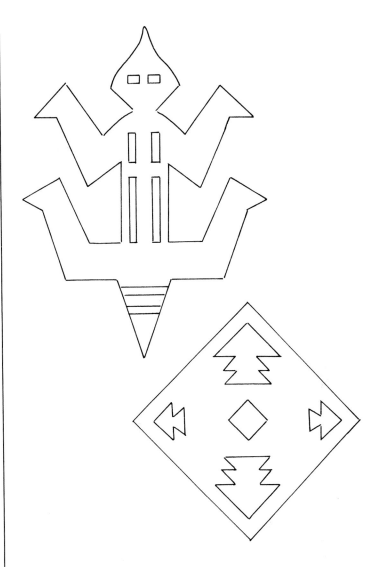

cal period of Navajo weaving was the chief pattern, used in the shoulder blankets worn by tribesmen. It had no significance in rank, and could be worn by any tribe member. It was often used for trading, especially among tribal leaders, and its name may derive from this practice. Unlike other Navajo weaving, the chief pattern is woven with the warp running the width rather than the length of the blanket. Its early designs were stripes, then nine rectangles were added to the striped ground, and finally, in its best-known version, the rectangles evolved into diamonds, with one large diamond centered on the blanket, quarter diamonds at the corners, and half diamonds at the mid-sides, all laid out on a striped field—a marriage of the basic Navajo stripe and diamond motifs.

The essentially geometric tradition of Navajo design was interrupted only with the introduction of pictorial blankets, which depicted in a naïve, abstract way animals, birds, men, houses, and other objects. The letters of the alphabet, taken from signs and commercial packages at the trading posts, were later incorporated as design elements. Some of the most interesting pictorial blankets display representations of Navajo divinities, called *yeis*, which are copied from sacred sand paintings. The figures are not ceremonial but decorative.

While the Navajo women were developing their distinctive art form, the Navajo men continued to raid their neighbors. Eventually their plunderings became so serious that in 1863 Kit Carson was sent to subdue them. Within a few months, he had rounded up the tribe of 10,000 and marched them 300 miles to an encampment in east central New Mexico where they were kept for five years. Bosque Redondo, the Navajo term for both the place and the captivity, essentially ended the first great era of weaving.

When the Navajos returned to their homelands in 1868, they had to rebuild their flocks of sheep to produce wool for weaving, and create a more peaceful way of life. What actually had the most far-reaching effect on them was the rail-

Two 20th-century adaptations of the chief pattern
blanket, both in red, white, and black.

Above, woven for the floor, about 6 feet square.
Photo courtesy Doris Leslie Blau.

Opposite page, an interpretation by Bertha Shaw,
1968. 3′10¾″ by 3′10″.
Photo courtesy U.S. Department of the Interior, Indian Arts and Crafts Board.

Eye-Dazzler, 1885–1895, a characteristic design using flat repetitious forms in bright colors and outlined in a contrasting color to create a dizzying effect. The aniline dyed colors are dark and light green, orange red, orange yellow, red, white, and black. 5'11½" by 4'½". *Photo courtesy Los Angeles County Museum of Art and Anthony Berlant, Santa Monica.*

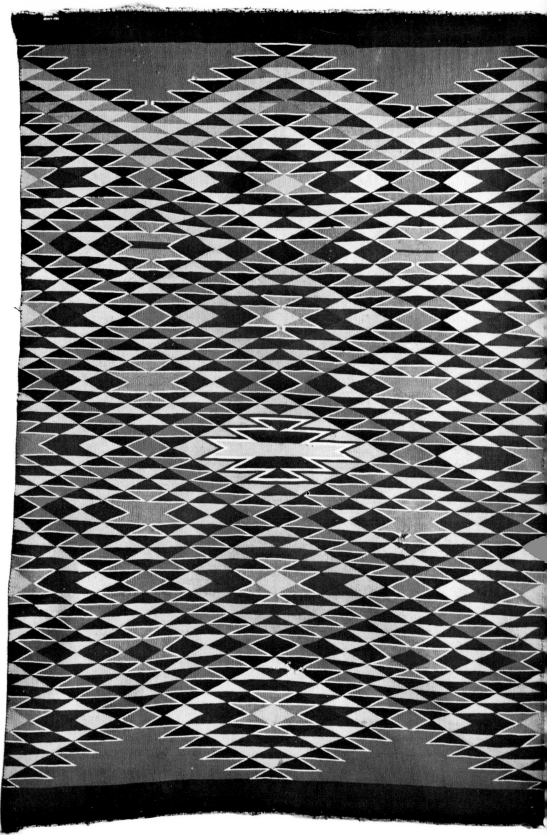

road, which pushed through to New Mexico and Arizona in the 1880s, bringing commercial traders and tourists in its cinder wake. Both radically changed the direction of Navajo weaving.

At the newly established trading posts, traders sold commercial American yarn and the recently developed aniline dyes. These dyes soon replaced indigo blue and vegetable dyes because they were easy to use and offered a wide range of colors, even though some colors were harsh and garish and faded easily.

Homespun tinted with aniline, and the commercial Germantown yarn already dyed in many colors, tempted the Navajos to incorporate as many colors as possible into one design, often to a dizzying, eye-assaulting effect. In what were aptly called eye-dazzlers, design elements were sometimes outlined in a contrasting color, and diagonal lines with serrated edges were often used to heighten the visual effect of intense contiguous colors. Diamonds kaleidoscopically broken into component geometric forms became important.

In addition to commercial yarns and dyes, the traders also brought in cheap machine-made blankets and yard goods, which replaced woven fabric for clothing. So toward the end of the century the Navajos stopped weaving blankets for their own use and turned their looms to the production of salable rugs, which the new railroad shipped to an eager rug-buying market on the East Coast. Their design began to be influenced by the traders, who thought they knew what their eastern customers wanted: a muted color scheme, limited to natural wool colors plus red, and a border to frame the design—elements made familiar by oriental carpets.

By the 1920s the quality of Navajo weaving had declined to such an extent that there were serious efforts by a few people to recapture some of its past excellence. Certain commercial yarns and aniline dyes were banned, wool was spun more carefully, and closer attention was urged in design and weaving techniques.

Rugs began to have regional characteristics as

Two Gray Hills pattern, 1965, interpreted by Julia Deal in natural colored wool of white, black, grays, and tan. 3'8¾" by 2'7¼". *Photo courtesy U.S. Department of the Interior, Indian Arts and Crafts Board.*

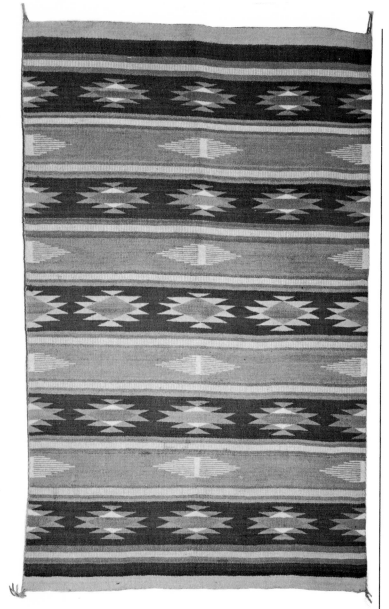

Typical Chinle design woven about 1960 in vegetal dyed wool. 4'6" by 2'10¼". *Photo courtesy U.S. Department of the Interior, Indian Arts and Crafts Board.*

distinctive styles were woven in different areas of the Navajo reservation, sometimes at the direction of a trading post owner, sometimes at the inspiration of an individual weaver. Here are some of the most popular contemporary designs, some new, others reaching back for their inspiration to the great classic era of the mid-nineteenth century.

Two Gray Hills. Named after a trading post in northwestern New Mexico, these are complicated yet balanced geometric designs surrounded by solid or figured borders. The wool is primarily natural colored—brown, black, white, with gray and tan made by spinning together black and brown fibers with white. Occasionally red or yellow or blue is used sparingly.

Teec Nos Pos. Geometric designs often incorporating the outlining technique of the late nineteenth century. They are similar to Two Gray Hills type but use much brighter colors.

Wide Ruins and *Chinle.* Banded, borderless rugs with geometric motifs within some of the wide stripes. They are woven in soft pastel colors in vegetable-dyed homespun. Aniline dyes are occasionally used in Chinle weaving.

Ganado and *Klagetoh.* Geometric designs are bordered and the characteristic color is the dark Ganado red, with black, gray, and white.

Yei. Elongated, stylized figures drawn from sacred sand paintings, which are woven in the northeastern part of the reservation.

Storm pattern. Woven around Tuba City in the western end of the Navajo reservation in black, white, gray, and red, this design has a central square, from which emanate four zigzag lines which reach out to four smaller squares at the corners.

Yei wall hanging, 1968, by Della Woody, with characteristic elongated and stylized figures. 19½″ by 19¾″. *Photo courtesy U.S. Department of the Interior, Indian Arts and Crafts Board.*

Color

Early weavings used the natural colors of wool —white, black, brown—and the grays and tans that could be spun from them, with red and blue, and some green and yellow. Imported Saxony yarns enlarged the color range, although favored hues were red, blue, green, and white. Aniline dyes introduced a full color spectrum, including purples, orange, and yellow-greens. Revival styles returned to more muted colors of vegetable dyes, like green, yellow, and coral.

Rugmaking Technique

All Navajo weaving is done on a vertical loom, usually hung from a ceiling or horizontal beam. The warp threads were strung between two poles and the weft threads passed alternately in front of and behind every other warp thread, thus creating a simple tapestry weave. By the end of the nineteenth century the more complicated twill and double weaves were introduced, but throughout the great rugweaving period of the nineteenth century the Navajos used the plain tapestry weave.

To approximate the flat weave of the Navajos, use the Gobelin stitch on needlepoint canvas (*see* Chapter 17).

Early American

America's contribution to rugmaking is undoubtedly the hooked rug. Some authorities trace hooking to ancient Egypt, others to Scandinavia and then to England from where the craft was brought to American by early settlers. But whether or not this distinctive technique actually originated on the northeastern shores of North America, it certainly reached its peak of creative expression and technical achievement in New England and the Maritime provinces of Canada.

Hooked rugs were not the only kind of floor coverings favored by the settlers. Wealthy colonists brought with them, or imported, oriental and European carpets. The rest of the population had to make their own, and for that they relied on Yankee ingenuity. Customarily the women spun and wove clothing and bed coverlets. When the woven goods were outgrown or outworn, the thrifty housewives gave them a second life by cutting them into thin strips out of which they made different kinds of floor coverings.

Rag rugs were one early form. The strips of cloth were joined lengthwise and wound into a ball. This became one continuous weft thread to be woven over and under the cotton or linen warp threads of a loom. Because of the shape of the loom, the resulting rag rugs were long and narrow; several had to be joined to make one large rug.

Braided rugs were also favored. Here the strips

Conventional abstract floral design with
a star center hooked in cotton and wool
on burlap using rose, orange, pink,
green, light and dark blue on a black
background. 39½" by 19". *Photo courtesy
Index of American Design, National
Gallery of Art, Washington, D.C.*

of cloth were plaited together, usually using three but sometimes as many as twelve strips in a braid. The braid was then wound flat in a circle or oval, occasionally in a square or rectangle, as large as desired, and the sides of the braid sewed to the adjoining piece of braid.

Scraps of cloth also formed the body of other kinds of rugs. In patchwork rugs snippets of dyed cloth were sewed on a dark piece of homespun woolen, making a colorful but not very durable floor covering. In Shaker rugs the scraps of rags were threaded together like a necklace, then densely sewn in geometric forms or abstract designs onto a strong backing. Other types of rugs also brought warmth and comfort to the colonial home—knitted, crocheted, and button rugs—but none had the importance of the hooked rug.

Great interest in hooking began in New England in the middle of the eighteenth century. Colonial women hooked rugs for both comfort and luxury, stitching into the canvas backings a variety of designs. Some were abstract and geometric forms, many were flowers and leaves in all kinds of arrangements, and some were pictorial representations of familiar scenes, historic events, and emblems of patriotic Americana, all charmingly naïve in their lack of perspective and simplicity.

A great variety of color was used in hooking—reds, blues, greens, black, white, rich brown, tans, grays, rose—and all of it came from the available cloth. If a piece of cloth did not yield enough strips of matching color to complete a design, the rug took on an equally delightful quilted or patchwork effect, although occasionally the women tried to dye the cloth, using berries, grapes, tree barks, roots, and other natural dyes.

While colonial women were enthusiastically stitching on the mainland, their sailors were hooking away the long days at sea, often using designs they had seen in European ports which further enriched the variety of rug patterns. Unwittingly, these seafarers helped promote the popularity of rug hooking.

By the middle of the nineteenth century inter-

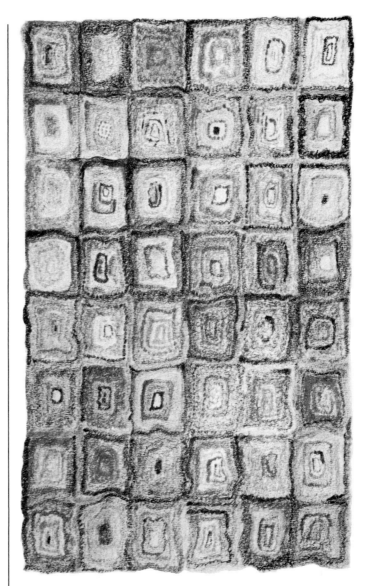

Geometric rug from Maine hooked of cotton and wool in the late 18th or early 19th century. The squares are in gray, brown, yellow, red, black, and violet. 6'10" by 4'2". *Photo courtesy Index of American Design, National Gallery of Art, Washington, D.C.*

Floral designs of every kind were favored. *Above*, center floral medallion in red and other colors on a brown ground surrounded by a ring of gray. 6'2½" by 6'1". *Opposite, top*, sprigs of flowers surrounding a pink horseshoe, symbol of good luck, on a brown background. 24" by 17½". *Opposite, bottom*, a few pink blossoms on a cream field framed by a leafy beige and tan scroll and a dark brown border. 2' by 3'6". *All photos courtesy Index of American Design, National Gallery of Art, Washington, D.C.*

Domestic animals were popular subjects, as in this barnyard scene hooked in brown, green, and red. 2'2" by 3'. *Photo courtesy Index of American Design, National Gallery of Art, Washington, D.C.*

est in hooking was burgeoning, and its lasting popularity was assured by an unlikely patron, a tin peddler from Maine named E.S. Frost. Frost was a machinist whose ill health forced him to give up his indoor trade for the healthier outdoor life of an itinerant peddler. He traveled through Maine, New Hampshire, and Massachusetts, supplying a wide variety of household goods, from calico to tinware. All through his travels he saw women hooking rugs from patterns they had drawn on sacking. To capture this ready market, the shrewd Yankee trader devised a way of mass producing his own designs. At first he made stencils of single design motifs on small metal plates cut from the copper bottoms of wash boilers he had picked up from his customers. Then he made stencils of entire rug designs and applied them to better quality burlap than was easily available to his customers. Eventually he developed a method for stamping the rug designs in color.

There is some speculation about the actual origins of the Frost designs. He drew his inspiration from Scandinavian, Scottish, English, Irish, Acadian as well as early American designs, and even from orientals, which he called Turkish. Many were floral designs, some were animals. Undoubtedly, he created some of the patterns himself; others were probably copied from the rugs of his customers that he admired and collected. But his importance and influence does not rest on the quality of the designs, which vary, but on the development of the stencil technique which eventually spread the craft of rug hooking all across the country.

Design

Florals were the most prevalent patterns and appeared in a variety of forms—formal and informal, single leaves and buds, sprigs, bouquets, bunches, in baskets, as wreaths, in central medallions, and in borders either alone or intertwined with scrolls and vines. All the familiar flowers of the New England garden were transplanted to

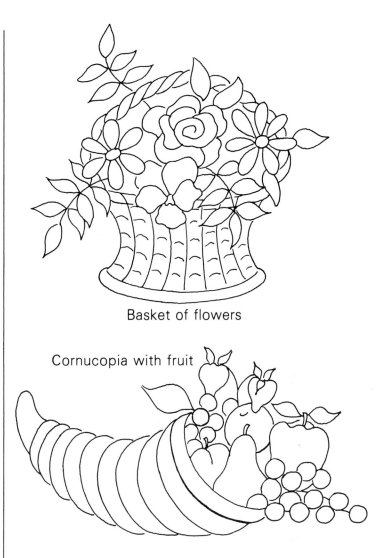

Basket of flowers

Cornucopia with fruit

the hooked rug—lilies, pansies, daisies, hollyhocks, and a profusion of pink and red roses.

Geometric and abstract designs appeared in abundance—basketweave, blocks, waves, zigzags, circles, triangles, and diamonds. Hit-or-miss was a random pattern derived from miscellaneous cloth scraps. The agate or mosaic pattern had wavy bands of color. Inch rugs were made of small blocks of different colors which developed their own pattern by the distribution of the colors. The box or log cabin pattern used L-shaped bands of different colors each grouped into a box. The shell design, also called scallop, tongue, and fish scale, placed half-ovals or semicircles in an overlapping design. Other geometric forms were lattice or trellis patterns, scrolls, the Roman key, and swastika motif, as well as good luck chain borders.

Pictorial designs were also popular. Seamen's wives often hooked replicas of their husbands' ships and incorporated anchors, waves, and stars. Landscapes depicted familiar scenes of church, home, farm, lake, or the river that flowed through town. Domestic and farm animals—cows, horses, chickens, ducks, lambs—often fill the landscapes. Great historical events were depicted, and patriotic themes were popular, like the American eagle and the flag. Slogans were stitched on doormats with messages to visitors: Welcome; Call Again; Good-bye.

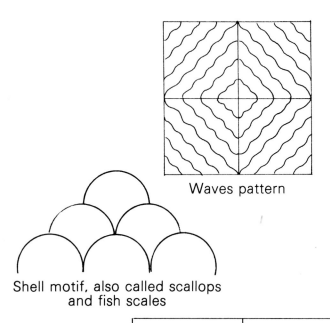

Waves pattern

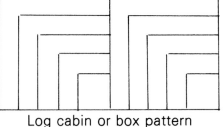

Shell motif, also called scallops
and fish scales

Log cabin or box pattern

American eagle

Patriotic motifs were often represented, such as this eagle and flag design hooked in 1838 in New Hampshire in red, blues, tans, browns, gray, plum, and maroon. 2′5½″ by 3′1½″. *Photo courtesy Index of American Design, National Gallery of Art, Washington, D.C.*

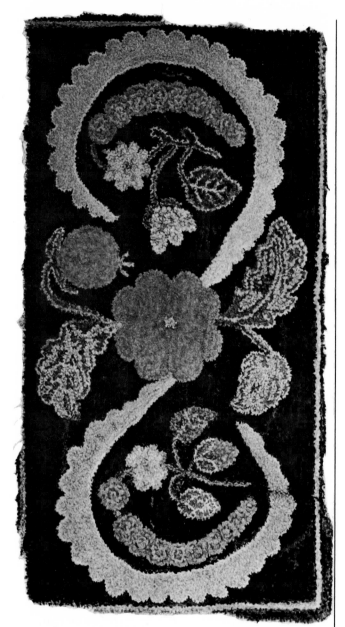

*Photo courtesy Index of American Design,
National Gallery of Art, Washington, D.C.*

Rugmaking Technique

Hand hooking involved pulling and pushing strips of cloth through a backing material of handwoven linen, cotton, or burlap. The backing had to be strong but coarse enough for easy manipulation. It was stretched over a wooden frame and the design marked on the backing in ink or charcoal.

The cloth strips were cut about ¼- or ½-inch wide from outworn woolen goods. In the early days they were cut by hand; commercial slitters were later used to produce uniform strips in various widths. Occasionally homespun yarn took the place of cloth strips. With a metal hook, usually a bent and sharpened nail, the hooking strips or yarn were drawn through the backing to form loops. They were raised about half an inch on the surface, generally left uncut, and were kept flat on the underside. Occasionally the background was trimmed around design motifs to make them stand out in relief.

To duplicate the early American technique of hand hooking, use punch hooking (*see* Chapter 20).

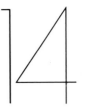

Contemporary American

Despite the popularity of hooked rugs through the nineteenth century and their unique contribution to the history of rugmaking, the hand weaving of carpets did not flourish in America. Unlike Europe, where the traditions of rug weaving reached back for centuries, there were few trained weavers in America. Domestic labor costs were high. Moreover, ever since the invention of the cotton gin, steam engine, and other industrial advances, America had turned its energies to producing by machine the goods it had formerly made by hand, and so the great contributions to rugmaking were technological.

The market was set by a large middle class with money to spend on household furnishings. At first a great part of their demand was met by importers who brought many fine rugs and carpets into the country from Europe. But this was a market that the domestic rug industry wished to fill. So Yankee ingenuity, coupled with a keen business eye, quickly created a mechanized carpet industry to supply the needs of the American people. A power loom was perfected, and by 1835 twelve weaving centers had been established in New England. They were aided by the tariff of 1824 which set a tax on woven imported carpet almost twice as high as that for imported raw wool, and later increased the difference even more.

Familiar names and companies appeared on

"Pow Wow," an abstract
wall rug designed by
Annie Bohlin. *Photo
courtesy Edward Fields,
Inc., New York.*

the scene. The Lowell Manufacturing Company, with three hand looms and twenty weavers from Scotland, produced ingrain carpet more quickly and cheaply than ever before. The factory foreman, Alexander Wright, and Erastus Brigham Bigelow spent years developing a power loom. When the loom finally began producing ingrain carpet it revolutionized the industry. By the middle of the century, Bigelow and his brother set up their own factory to power-loom a pile carpet, an elegant improvement over the cheaper ingrain produced at Lowell and prized by the middle class.

In the next hundred years the mechanized carpet industry grew, driving out not only most of the hand-weaving establishments but also those companies that did not keep up with new techniques of manufacturing and marketing. And so, despite some desire for hand-woven rugs, there were very few available. Toward the end of the nineteenth century two Germans set up looms they had brought with them from Europe and for twenty years made fine hand-knotted carpets in New York for a sophisticated market before they were driven out of business by the power looms. During the same period, a branch of the Royal Wilton Carpet Works of England made pile Axminster carpets in New Jersey for a short time. At Williamsbridge in The Bronx, New York, a factory was set up in 1893 to hand weave flat Aubusson-type wall hangings and upholstery fabrics and occasionally rugs, using primarily French designs.

While these few hand-weaving establishments tried to stay in business for a small, discriminating clientele, carpet manufacturers supplied their wares to eager customers who covered the floors not only of their private homes and offices, but also of the public rooms in hotels, theaters, and ocean liners. By this time the flat-woven ingrain carpet was replaced in popularity by the diverse textures of the Axminster, Wilton, velvet, and tapestry weaves. This boom in wall-to-wall carpeting and large room-sized rugs expanded to include smaller rugs which could be sent by mail, and a great part of carpet production was given over to the mail order business.

The burgeoning business spurred the search for new fibers. A substitute was eagerly sought for wool, which was imported from all parts of the world and often varied in quality, price, and availability. Rayon combined with cotton was the first man-made fiber to be used in carpets, producing a glossy luster that was immediately popular. But rayon presented problems in dyeing, soil resistance, and durability, so the industry looked further.

There was greater success with hydrocarbon-type fibers like Orlon, Saran, Dynel, and by the 1960s synthetic fibers, under different trade names, accounted for 85 per cent of carpet production. But the widespread use of synthetic carpeting spawned a reaction among more discriminating buyers who wanted better designed and more exclusive products. To accommodate them, some carpet manufacturers set up studios for custom work, other designers established small firms of their own. Two creative firms in custom carpet work are Edward Fields and Stanislav V'Soske.

Rather than offer handmade room-sized carpeting, which would be prohibitively expensive, to compete with machine-made broadloom, Fields originated the handmade area rug. It was specifically created to accommodate an arrangement of furniture on an otherwise bare floor. At first the chairs and sofas were planned to set on the edges of the rug, but later the furniture was often moved back to the bare floor to display the rug design more effectively.

Fields offers a variety of designs: floral, modern, classic, abstract, geometric, period designs, oriental adaptations. To provide an exclusive product, the sample designs are produced in the customer's choice of size and colors. They are all made of wool by the tufting technique, and occasionally incorporate different surface levels and areas of both cut and uncut loops.

The V'Soske firm actually developed and refined the method for speedy hand tufting which could produce a variety of textures with

"Maze," designed by
Roger McDonald and
inspired by an ancient
Aztec lace design. The
line design is actually
below the ground and
is defined by low
thick loops shorter
than the sheared pile
field. 4' by 6'. *Photo
courtesy V'Soske,
New York.*

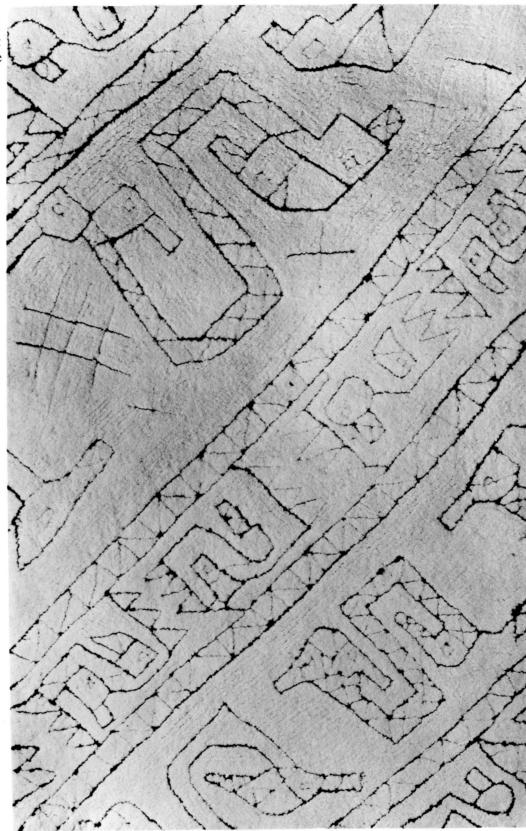

changes of needles. Different weights of wool are tufted to various heights, and the loops either sheared into pile or left uncut. Sometimes tightly twisted yarn contrasts with a looser twist, sometimes a line of low uncut loops is partially hidden in a field of higher cut pile, sometimes areas of sheared pile are steamed and combed for a furry look. In some rugs the pattern itself is created by the direction of the tufting, which can be stitched in straight lines, at angles, and in random patterns. And sometimes the designs are set off in relief by carving or incising the field.

V'Soske's innovative carpets rely not only on this vast array of textures, used singly and in combination, but also on a variety of designs that range from op, cubist and abstract to classic and oriental-derived. Some of them are the products of contemporary artists, like Stuart Davis and Arshile Gorky, and a few belong to museum collections.

Obviously the best of contemporary rugs and wall hangings have gone well beyond a utilitarian, and even merely decorative, purpose to become an art medium in themselves, reflecting the creative energies of our time. The designs of an impressive roster of contemporary artists are being translated into hand-woven rugs and tapestries in the traditional pile and flat-weave techniques. Unlike the rug designs of historical periods, these contemporary tapestries are not characterized by typical motifs, composition, or colors; they are uniquely personal expressions of individual artists. And like lithographs and other multiples, they are usually woven in limited editions, often between five and twenty, numbered and signed by the artist.

Under the careful supervision of Gloria F. Ross, a group of hangings are being made by hand in both flat-weave and hooked-rug techniques. Exhibited at Pace Editions Inc. gallery, they are designed by a number of contemporary artists who include her sister, Helen Frankenthaler, Robert Goodnough, Adolph Gottlieb, Robert Motherwell, Kenneth Noland, Louise Nevelson, Frank Stella, and Ernest Trova. Pro-

"Duncan," an assemblage of textures, shapes, and color areas created by a variety of contemporary hooking techniques, including incising, concave and convex raising and carving, fully looped areas, fully sheared areas, and partially sheared in different heights. 5' by 7'. *Photo courtesy V'Soske, New York.*

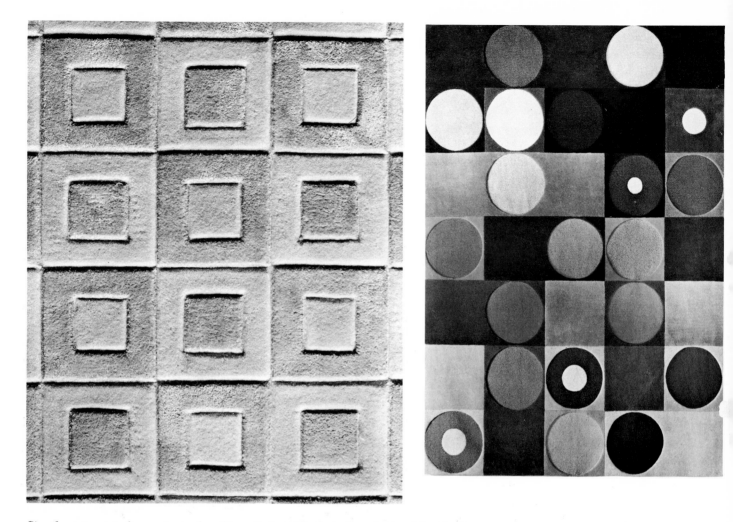

Simple geometric forms, incised and bevelled, create complex relationships. *Left*, a detail of "Fifty-Fifty," designed by Stanislav V'Soske, with pale mustard central squares surrounded by silvery green. *Right*, "Checkmate," designed by Paul V'Soske, with low-lying circles of uncut loops within blocks of higher sheared pile. 5′ by 7′. *Both photos courtesy V'Soske, New York.*

Limited edition flat-woven tapestries designed by two contemporary artists. *Above, Elegy to the Spanish Republic No. 116, 1970,* by Robert Motherwell. 7' by 9'. *Left, Red and Blue Abstraction,* 1970, by Robert Goodnough. 6'5" by 8'7". *Both photos courtesy Pace Editions, Inc., and Gloria F. Ross, New York.*

duced in close collaboration with artist and weaver, the tapestries utilize different fibers—mainly wool, but also linen and metallic threads—to recreate most precisely the artist's original intent. In a design by Louise Nevelson, for instance, it is the use of gold thread woven in varying heights and densities that captures the sculptural effect and depth of the form against the black ground; in a Robert Motherwell, the incorporation of linen fiber to get a really clear white.

The flat-weave hangings are made in Europe using the traditional tapestry technique, the hooked rug hangings in America utilizing a traditional punch-hooking method. Mrs. Ross at one time hooked the tapestries herself, often combining cut and uncut loops. Now the large hooked hangings, especially the institutional commissions, are given to master craftsmen for production.

Whereas the Gloria F. Ross tapestries are all executed in a flat-woven or hooked technique, another group of hangings are being produced in hand-knotted wool and silk pile under the aegis of the Charles E. Slatkin, Inc., Galleries. Called Modern Master Tapestries, the series is based on the designs of a group of European painters, including Jean (Hans) Arp, Jean Cocteau, Paul Klee, Fernand Léger, Joan Miró, and Pablo Picasso, and a large group of American painters of the 60s, including Milton Avery, Leonard Baskin, Alexander Calder, Jim Dine, Robert Indiana, Roy Lichtenstein, Ben Shahn, Saul Steinberg, and Andy Warhol. Fascinated with the possibilities of the medium, some of the artists utilize an evenly cut pile, others, like Theodoros Stamos, call for a variety of pile depth, shorn at different levels. All use the traditional pile rug technique, transforming it for their personal creative expression.

Rugmaking Technique

Modern tufting is done on closely woven cotton duck strung taut over a frame. The design is drawn on the back of the material and the design punched from the back, using various kinds of tufting needles threaded with continuous yarn. The height of the loop and other technical adjustments are made in the tools to produce the desired surface and texture. Tufting can be done in straight or wavy lines, at angles, in circles, and in random patterns, all affecting the look of the finished surface. All finishing operations—shearing, carving, incising—are done by hand after the tufting process is completed.

The traditional pile-and flat-weave Aubusson techniques are described in Chapter 9.

To duplicate tufting, use punch hooking (*see* Chapter 20). It is essentially the same technique as the tufting methods used by contemporary rug makers.

To approximate the flat tapestry weave, use the Gobelin stitch on needlepoint canvas (*see* Chapter 17).

To approximate the pile surface, use Turkey tufting on needlepoint canvas (*see* Chapter 17) or latch hooking (*see* Chapter 18).

Contemporary Techniques

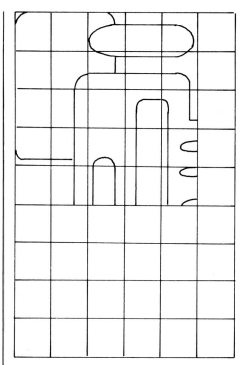

How to Use This Book

Happily for contemporary craftsmen, the often elaborate and time-consuming techniques of our ancestors have been improved and streamlined. And while it is still possible, of course, to make rugs and hangings on hand-operated looms in the authentic techniques of the past, it is also possible to utilize up-to-date tools and methods that can replicate the designs and often the textures of the original works, whether they are the tufted rugs of the Orient, Spain, England, or France, the flat-woven kilims of the east, the Aubussons of France and Navajo weavings, the early American hooked rugs, or the Scandinavian ryas.

The most important improvement in rugmaking methods is the availability of all kinds of backing materials, from coarse mesh canvas to tightly woven cotton duck. It is no longer necessary to weave the backing itself; commercial goods are now available to support any kind of surface texture from a flat tapestry weave to a long shaggy pile simply by stitching, hooking, pulling, or pushing the appropriate yarn into the appropriate backing.

Hand in hand with the availability of a wide range of backing materials is the development of efficient hand-held tools and improved yarns. Modern punch and speed needles have replaced the sharpened and curved nail with which our forefathers hooked their rugs. A specially engineered latch hook has supplanted the crochet hook formerly used to make cut pile rugs. Yarns are now uniformly spun, moth-proofed, and dyed in a dazzling array of colors and shades in matched dye lots.

Four Contemporary Techniques

A successful rug or hanging is the happy marriage of the design and its method of production. Some designs are more appropriately executed in one technique than another, so a brief understanding of the general characteristics of each method is essential, even before selecting the pattern itself. Detailed instructions for each technique follow in chapters 17 through 21.

Needlepoint is the most versatile method. Its variety of stitches can produce a flat or tufted pile surface, either cut or uncut. And because canvas density ranges from coarse to very fine you can accommodate designs of virtually any scale and intricacy, even the most detailed oriental patterns which require 400 stitches per square inch. Moreover, the color range of needlepoint yarn is exceptionally wide and varied enough to meet the most exacting color requirements.

Needlepoint has the additional advantage of portability; it is light in weight and large rugs are often made in easily carried sections.

Latch hooking produces a rich, uniformly sheared pile on a coarse mesh canvas which commonly has 16 or at most 25 stitches per square inch. The coarseness of the canvas makes it suitable for bold, angular designs; only large free curves can be satisfactorily rendered. While a cut pile surface can also be made by rya, punch hooking, and Turkey tufting on needlepoint canvas, the fastest and easiest way to produce a dense, even pile is by using the precut yarns and special tools of latch hooking.

Portability is not an outstanding characteristic of latch hooking. The dense pile often makes the project too heavy to carry.

Rya is a method of knotting yarn on a specially woven backing which forms 6 stitches of shaggy pile to the square inch. Because of the sparseness of the stitching, it is best suited to largely drawn design elements. Subtly shaded areas of color, however, are possible because each stitch requires several strands of yarn, each of which can be a different color or a different shade of the same color. Rya pile is often 2½ to 3 inches long. It can be left looped, and when cut it is sheared unevenly, in contrast to latch hooked pile which is about one inch long and evenly sheared.

Rya knotting covers the backing fairly quickly, but is not easily portable since the backing itself is heavy, even before it is stitched.

Punch hooking can produce widely varied surface textures. You can punch loops of various heights in thin or thick yarn and leave them cut or uncut, and you can bevel the stitches to create a rounded profile. Moreover, you can combine any or all of these textural effects in the same rug or wall hanging.

Punch hooking also lends itself particularly well to curvilinear shapes because the stitches are applied to a tightly woven backing in any desired sequence—in curves, lines, zigzags, diagonally, horizontally, vertically. This is in contrast with needlepoint and latch hooking which must conform to the horizontal–vertical grid of the canvas. For this reason, punch hooking is especially appropriate for pictorial designs. The actual stitching—25 to 30 loops per square inch—is comparatively sparse, but its flexible and flowing nature makes possible fairly intricate designs.

Since punch hooking must be done on a frame, it is not at all portable.

Choosing the Right Technique

Selecting an appropriate technique involves an understanding not only of the capabilities of each technique, but also of the desired characteristics of the finished project. If you want to emphasize clarity of design, choose one of the flat needlepoint stitches. If you treasure texture over pattern, and particularly enjoy the look and feel of a deep pile, work in rya or latch hooking. If you prefer a looped rather than a sheared surface, try the varied possibilities of punch hooking.

If you prize authenticity, follow the techniques suggested at the end of each chapter of Section I. However, in searching for the most authentic reproduction of a period design, you may have to balance fidelity of pattern with fidelity of texture. As you will see, the knotted pile of a coarsely woven rug can be reproduced by various methods, but it is not feasible to produce a pile texture denser than 100 stitches per square inch (Turkey tufting on needlepoint canvas). However, at the sacrifice of the pile surface, you can reproduce extremely fine and detailed designs using one of the flat needlepoint stitches.

Other factors may dictate your choice of rug technique. If you plan to lay your rug in an area of heavy traffic, consider a pile surface to protect the backing from excessive wear. If the pleasure in making a rug is being able to work on it wherever you go, choose needlepoint for its portability.

Rug Designs

Your general understanding of the different rugmaking techniques will help you select one of the thirty rug designs illustrated in A Portfolio of Design Adaptations in Section III. Each design is presented in two forms—graphed to indicate exact stitching, and pictorially to indicate color changes by the various shades of gray. You will probably find it helpful to refer to both representations during various aspects of your rugmaking. As you can see from the pictorial representations, each design carries suggested colors that reproduce a typical color scheme for that period rug. However, should your home or your own taste dictate an entirely different color selection, create and substitute your own palette.

In addition to the thirty full rug designs, there are many line drawings of period motifs scattered throughout Section I. They can be substituted for the motifs incorporated in the full rug designs, or they can be used in needlework pillows or other accessories. For enlarging and transferring these motifs, apply the instructions given in Chapter 16 for enlarging and transferring the full rug designs.

From Design to Backing

Having chosen a design and technique for your rug or wall hanging, you are ready to put the design on your backing material. But first read the chapter devoted to a full explanation of your particular stitching method: for needlepoint, see Chapter 17; for latch hooking, Chapter 18; for rya, Chapter 19; and for punch hooking, Chapter 20.

Enlarging the Design

Obviously even the smallest rug or hanging is going to be larger than the pages of this book, so your design will have to be enlarged to your finished size. You can do this by photostating, using the pictorial representation of the design; by counting, using the graphed design; or by the box method. Whichever method you use, the proportions of the finished project will be the same as in the design.

Photostating is the simplest way of getting a life-sized drawing of your rug pattern so you can actually transfer it to your backing material. It can be used with any of the stitching techniques.

To have a photostat made, take this book to a photo copier (listed in the classified pages of the telephone book) and ask for a stat of a rug design made to your specifications. Use the pictorial,

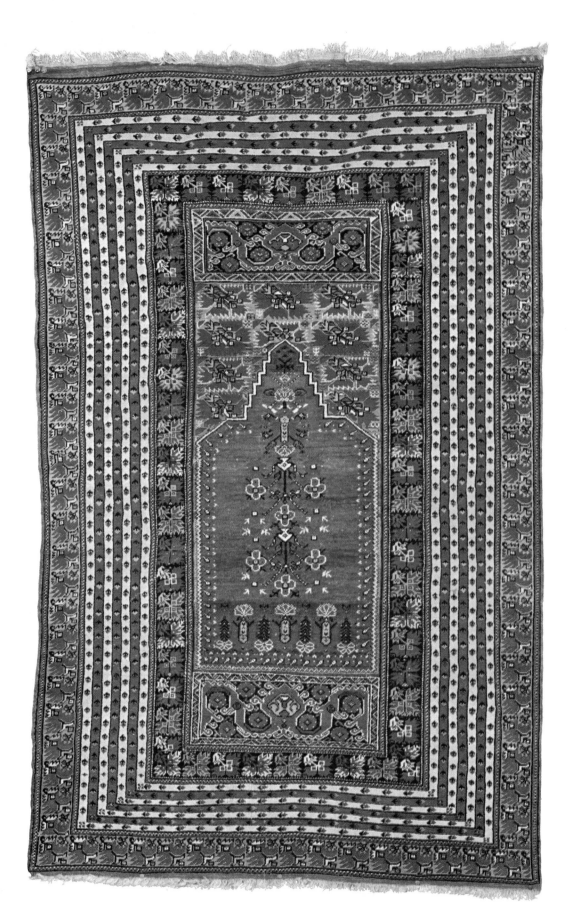

A Ghiordes prayer rug of unusual beauty balancing color and form. A cascade of flowers hangs from the point of the *mihrab,* which is surrounded by multi-borders of flowers and leaves.

Photo courtesy
Sotheby & Co., London

Two Persian medallion rugs of contrasting backgrounds. *Right:* A Hamadan village rug whose central medallion and bird and flower design are laid on a buff-colored field of natural camel's hair. *Opposite:* A magnificent silk medallion rug from the first half of the sixteenth century whose central eight-pointed star is surrounded by white cloud bands and a variety of flowers in white, yellow and green and encircled by a main border of palmettes and peonies. 7 feet 11 inches by 5 feet 5 inches.

Photo this page courtesy Kent-Costikyan, Inc., New York; photo opposite page courtesy National Gallery of Art, Washington, D.C. (Widener Collection)

Three Caucasian rugs. *Right:* Detail of a Karabagh woven in the southern Caucasus with an unusual parrot design. The floral border shows a French influence and the dimensions mark it as a *kelleye,* or long runner. 16 feet 5 inches by 6 feet 3 inches. *Below:* A typical Kazak design featuring an octagonal medallion, with latch hooks and eight-pointed stars. 7 feet 7 inches by 6 feet 6 inches. *Below right:* A characteristic Chichi rug with wide border of stylized flowers and slanted bands surrounding a well-filled field of small octagons ornamented with tiny latch hooks. 4 feet 9 inches by 3 feet 9 inches.

Photos courtesy Perez (London) Ltd.

A Caucasian rug from the Kuba region using the ram's horn motif and a variety of rosettes, animals and geometric forms in a characteristically angular treatment.

A typical Ladik prayer rug with five stylized tulips surmounting a plain red *mihrab* field. It is dated 1216 AH (in the year of the hegira or A.D. 1801). 6 feet 7 inches by 4 feet 3 inches.

Photo courtesy Perez (London) Ltd.

Left: A Princess Bokhara or Tekke prayer rug, called a *katchli* or *hatchlie*, whose prayer niche is intersected by a cross and filled with typical blue candelabra figures. 5 feet by 3 feet 11 inches.
Below: A fine Ghiordes prayer rug with typically delicate coloring, free-standing columns and narrow floral borders which incorporates an unusual village scene at the bottom. Woven around 1800.
Below left: A large Indo-Chinese rug with lotus flowers and sprays made in the nineteenth century after an early seventeenth century Buddhist design of Indian origin. The main border uses a swastika motif linked in a continuous pattern and signifying endless luck.

Photo on left courtesy Perez (London) Ltd.;
photos below and below left courtesy Doris Leslie Blau

Opposite: A lovely Samarkand weaving showing strong Chinese influences in the medallions and wave and cloud band borders. 7 feet 9 inches by 4 feet 7 inches. *Below:* A Samarkand *saph,* or multiple prayer rug, in which the same border and stylized pomegranate tree growing out of a vase are woven in different colors on various colored fields in each of the seven compartments. 13 feet 4 inches by 3 feet 7 inches. *Left:* An unusual Chinese pillar rug in which the five-clawed imperial dragons are standing rather than horizontally entwined around a column. The lower border uses a characteristic wave motif. 8 feet 1 inch by 4 feet 6 inches.

Photos opposite and below courtesy Perez (London) Ltd.;
photo left courtesy S. Franses, London

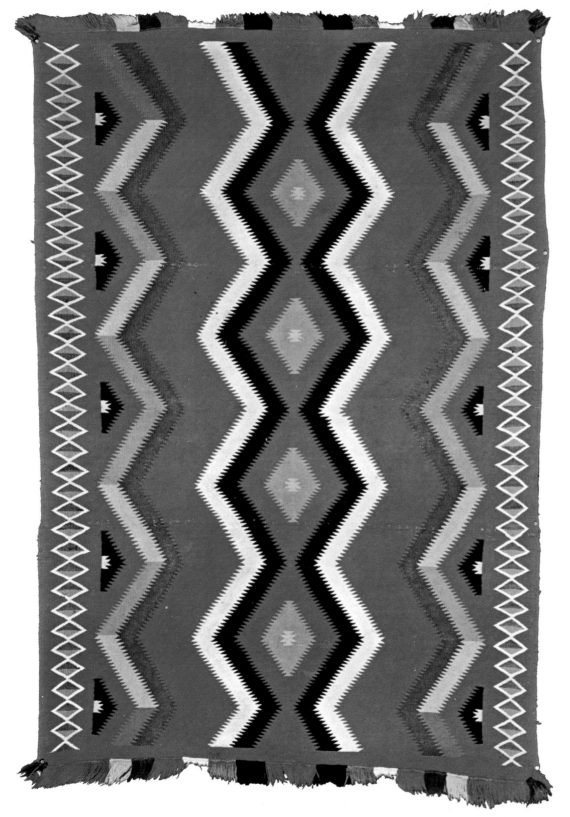

Three Navajo blankets. *Opposite:* A twentieth century weaving from the Steamboat area of northeastern Arizona, noted for its eight-point star designs. 6 feet by 3 feet 9 inches. *Center:* A chief pattern of the late nineteenth century with a central diamond on a striped field and half- and quarter-diamonds at the mid-sides and corners. 5 feet 1 inch by 3 feet 3 inches. *Left:* A small child's blanket with serrated chevrons, comparable in style and quality to larger Navajo weavings. Made of Germantown wool in the late nineteenth century. 4 feet 1 inch by 2 feet 11 inches.

Photos courtesy Doris Leslie Blau, New York

Two nineteenth century hooked rug designs. *Right:* Geometric forms and flowers hooked in cotton and wool in Pennsylvania. 3 feet 2 inches by 3 feet 10 inches. *Below:* A variety of brilliantly colored blooms from an early American garden fenced in by a black and red chain border. 5 feet 2 inches by 2 feet 11 inches.

Photos courtesy Index of American Design, National Gallery of Art, Washington, D.C.

Two vivid poppies hand tufted in wool, then sheared to various heights, with carved and beveled edges for added texture and richness. Designed by Robert Riddle and called "Amapolas."

Photo courtesy V'Soske, Inc., New York

Below: The strong, bold design and optical emphasis of "Coming to a Point" is heightened by incising the sheared wool tufting around the circles and beveling their edges. By Herbert Bayer. *Right:* "Lizard," designed in 1904 by the painter Akseli Gallen-Kallela, the pioneer of modern Finnish ryamaking, is an example of the Jugend style. It was inspired by the Finnish national epic in which a terrible lizard, coiled and bloody, sits on the banks of the River of Death.

Photo below courtesy V'Soske, Inc., New York;
photo at right courtesy Finnish Society of Crafts and Design, Helsinki

Left: "Appletree," a contemporary Finnish rya by artist Norma Heimola, 1969. *Below:* "July," designed and woven by Eva Brummer, noted rya innovator, who sought to capture the softness and richness of color found in the great folk ryas. *Bottom left:* An early bridal rya incorporating the tree of life, the bridal couple and animals. *Bottom center:* A splendid star motif bridal rya woven in 1815 whose rich effect derives from the various shades of blue and red. *Bottom right:* A wheel motif reminiscent of the eight-pointed star of early folk ryas is used by artist Ritva Puotila in "Ares," a contemporary weaving.

Photo at far left courtesy Friends of Finnish Handicraft, Helsinki; all others courtesy Finnish Society of Crafts and Design, Helsinki

Wall hangings designed by three contemporary artists and executed in three different techniques. *Below:* Adolph Gottlieb's "Black Signs," a tufted hanging made by punch hooking. 4 feet 6 inches by 6 feet. *Far right:* Frank Stella's "Flin Flon XIII 1970," a flat woven hanging. 8 feet 10 inches square. *Bottom:* Roy Lichtenstein's "Modern Tapestry," a sheared pile weaving. 8 feet 10 inches by 12 feet 3 inches.

Photos at right courtesy Pace Editions, Inc., New York; photo below courtesy Charles E. Slatkin Galleries, New York, copyright Modern Master Tapestries

rather than the graphed, representation of the design and request a positive stat or you will probably receive the negative, which will have the white and black lines in reverse. Single photostats are available in sizes up to about 40 by 60 inches; if your rug exceeds those dimensions, you can have separate stats pieced together.

Counting from the graph is an alternate, and economical, way of enlarging the design, but it is useful only for needlepoint and latch hooking where the square mesh of the canvas corresponds to the squared boxes of the graph. In the graphed design each box can represent as many stitches as you want, as long as each box *always* represents the same number of stitches, both horizontally and vertically.

To determine how many stitches to assign to each box, correlate the finished size of the rug with the size canvas you are using. For example say your design is 80 boxes wide, you are using latch hook canvas of 4 mesh to the inch, and you want your finished project to be 40 inches wide. If you assigned one stitch to each box, the 80 boxes would require 80 stitches. And since 4 stitches on your latch hook canvas equals one inch, the 80 stitches would measure 20 inches. Since you want your rug or hanging to be 40 inches wide, or twice as wide, you should assign two stitches to each box.

To give another illustration, suppose you are using Number 10 needlepoint canvas which has 10 stitches to the inch instead of the latch hooking canvas. You are using the same design, which is 80 boxes wide, and you still want your rug to be 40 inches wide. If you assigned one stitch to each box, the 80 boxes would require 80 stitches, but on your needlepoint canvas those 80 stitches would now only measure 8 inches. Since you want your project to be 40 inches wide, or five times as wide, you must assign five stitches to each box. As you can see, you can enlarge the design either by increasing the number of stitches each box represents, or by using a larger mesh canvas, in which case the same number of stitches would take up more space and thus increase the dimensions.

If you find that counting from the graph is a tedious way to enlarge a big rug, you may want to photostat the whole design and transfer the outlines to your rug backing, then work the individual motifs stitch by stitch from the graph. If your design or border is geometric and depends on a precise stitch count, close attention to the graph is essential.

The box method is another alternate way of enlarging the design. It can be used with any of the rugmaking techniques and avoids what may be costly photostating fees for large rugs. However, the resulting freehand copy is less accurate than either of the two other enlarging procedures. Follow these steps:

1. On a sheet of paper copy your rug design from these pages. You can do this by tracing it onto a sheet of tracing paper. Or you can have the page reproduced mechanically, either by a duplicating machine or, if the result is not clear enough, by photostat (a page-sized photostat is reasonable in cost).

2. Rule the traced or copied design into squares (*see* Figure 1). Make ½- or 1-inch boxes if your design is fairly simple; use much smaller squares if your design is intricate.

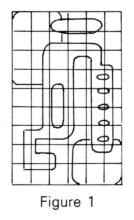

Figure 1

3. Now prepare a large sheet of paper with the outlines of your finished rug or hanging. Grid this large sheet with exactly the same number of

squares and in the same arrangement as you have on your design. For instance, if your small design runs 6 boxes horizontally and 9 vertically for a total of 54 boxes, duplicate the same grid on your large sheet. You can see that, although there are the same number of boxes on both sheets, they are much larger on the rug-sized pattern.

4. Copy your design freehand onto the large sheet of paper, square by square, working from one small box of the design to the larger corresponding box of the actual pattern (*see* Figure 2).

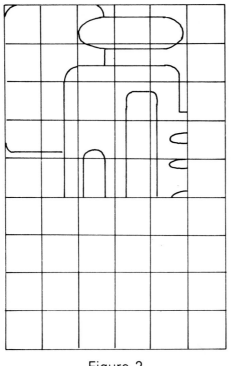

Figure 2

Putting the Design on the Backing

The method of actually transferring the design from the photostat or drawing onto the rug backing will depend on what stitching technique you are using. The open mesh of needlepoint and latch hooking allows enough visibility for tracing the pattern, while the closely woven fabric backings for rya and punch hooking do not.

Transfer to needlepoint and latch hooking canvas. The pattern on the photostat or freehand drawing should be as bold as possible. If the lines seem indistinct, darken them with an indelible marker. For maximum visibility, place the design face up on a white table top or on a white sheet on the floor. Lay the rug canvas over it and tape them together. The white background will enable you to see the design through the mesh of the canvas. Trace the design onto the canvas with an indelible waterproof marker.

If you are stitching your needlepoint or hooked project in more than one piece, remember that the selvage of the canvas must run vertically on all the sections so you can make neat joins later, and that you must allow the designated seam allowance on all the sections. The easiest way to do this is to plan out your rug sections right on the design drawing. The sections need not all be the same size; the divisions can fall at the most expedient places, usually in the middle of a motif or between the border and the field. Then cut the design, drawing up, into stitching sections and transfer the design of each section to each piece of canvas. When planning the joins, try to make as few as possible, and if you can, avoid any four-way joins which are bulky and difficult to make.

Transfer to fabric backing for rya and punch hooking. The fabric backing used for rya or punch hooking is too densely woven to trace through it as you can with needlepoint and latch hooking canvas, so use one of the following methods to transfer the design. The design should be transferred to the face of the rya backing, but since the punch hooked backing is the same on both sides, it doesn't matter on which side the pattern is drawn.

1. Perforation method. On the photostat or design drawing, outline the pattern with a series of pinholes, or trace over the design with a tailor's perforating wheel. Lay the design paper over the rug backing and trace over the perforated lines with an indelible waterproof marker so that a series of dots is transferred to the backing, form-

ing the design outline from which to work.

2. Gauze method. Place a piece of gauze over the photostat or design drawing and trace the rug pattern on it with an indelible waterproof marker. Then place the gauze on the backing and retrace the pattern with the same indelible waterproof marker. The fine mesh of the gauze allows enough ink to be transferred to the backing to form an outline from which to work.

3. Hot iron transfer method. Outline the design on the photostat or drawing with a hot iron transfer pencil, then place the design sheet *face down* on the backing and press it with a hot iron. Work with a sharp copying pencil and keep your iron hot enough to transfer the dye of the pencil without scorching the backing. The thicker the paper, the longer the dye takes to penetrate, so rotate the iron slowly.

On a rya backing the pattern will be transferred in reverse because the design is placed face down, but for punch hooking, the pattern will not appear as a mirror image on the surface because the punch technique of working from the back of the fabric corrects the reversal. Similarly the designs transferred by the perforation and the gauze methods would be reversed in a punch hooking and right side up in a rya. This reversal makes no difference in any of the designs in this book. However, if you are going to stitch in your name, initials, or a date, correct the reversal.

Color Guide

You will want a color indicator as you work. You can color your photostat or drawing with crayons, or simply pencil in the names of the colors. If you don't want to carry the paper pattern around with you, tag your backing with pieces of colored yarn in the appropriate areas. On needlepoint or latch hook canvas you can actually paint the entire design with acrylics, but the more densely woven rya and punch hooked backings tend to stiffen and clog if painted.

17

Needlepoint

Backing Material

Needlepoint is stitched on specially woven canvas, usually made of cotton, which has clearly separated horizontal and vertical threads. When the threads are closely paired, the canvas is called penelope; when the threads are equally spaced, the canvas is known as mono. Many different stitches can be made on either canvas, but some are only successful on one or the other.

Both penelope and mono canvas are identified by the number of stitching threads per running inch. For example, Number 7 canvas has seven single or seven double threads per linear inch; Number 10 canvas has ten single or ten double threads per linear inch. Canvas is generally available in widths of 36, 40, and 54 inches.

The type of canvas you choose to work on will depend to some extent on the stitch you are using. The basketweave and Soumak stitches can be made either on mono or penelope canvas; the Gobelin stitch is most successful on mono canvas; and the cross stitch and Turkey tufting need to be locked into the double construction of penelope canvas.

The size mesh canvas you select will be dictated by the complexity of your pattern. The more intricate and detailed the design is, the higher the mesh count must be to accommodate it. But remember that any canvas denser than

Number 12 or Number 14—which can produce 144 or 196 stitches per square inch—will be tedious to work in a rug-sized project. On the other hand, if your design is fairly bold, take advantage of a low-mesh, quick-stitching canvas like Number 5. An excellent all-purpose canvas is Number 7 or Number 10. On either one you can produce fairly detailed motifs and still cover the canvas rapidly enough to keep your enthusiasm from flagging.

Before cutting your canvas for work, plan your design layout. The selvages of the canvas should be at the side of the work, that is, they should run vertically. When making a project in more than one piece, it is especially important that the selvages run the same way—vertically—on all canvas sections so that you can make precisely matched joins when assembling them later (you will find that often the horizontal and vertical threads are not equidistant, even in what appears to be perfectly squared canvas mesh).

Cut the canvas 3 inches wider all around than your rug pattern. This 3-inch seam allowance on all sides is necessary on every piece of canvas for later blocking, whether you are making a rug in one piece or in many sections to be joined later. Protect all cut edges with masking or fabric tape to avoid unraveling.

Yarn

Rugs, which demand the best and most durable yarns, should be made of wool. Wall hangings can incorporate virtually any kind of yarn or decorative fiber since they will not receive heavy wear. There are various kinds of wool yarn for needlepointing. Your choice will depend on the size canvas you are using and the availability of colors.

Persian wool is the most versatile of needlepoint yarns. It is available by the skein or ounce in a vast array of graduated shades. Each thread of Persian yarn consists of three loosely twisted strands which can easily be separated to use alone on fine mesh canvas or in combination with strands of other colors. Generally, use one full thread (that is, all three strands) on Number 10 and 12 canvases, use two of the three strands on Number 14 canvas, and one of the three strands on finer mesh. Double the thread (six strands) for Number 7 canvas, and use eight strands for Number 5 canvas. Increase your palette by combining strands of different colors in the same needle to create subtly shaded or boldly tweeded areas of color.

Tapestry yarn is a tightly twisted 4-ply yarn generally available in 40-yard skeins in a more limited color range than Persian yarn. Use one full thread on Number 10 canvas, double it for Number 7 canvas. It cannot be separated for finer canvas work.

Rya yarn, used primarily for rya work (*see* Chapter 19), is also effective for needlepoint, especially in the long-pile Turkey tufting stitch. It is a tightly twisted 2-ply yarn available in a fairly good range of graded colors and in two weights. Use one strand of the lighter weight yarn on Number 10 canvas, double it on Number 7 canvas; use one strand of the heavier yarn on Number 7 canvas. Neither can be separated for finer canvas work.

Rug wool is a heavy yarn available in a variety of slightly different weights and plies to fit the coarser mesh canvases. It is offered by different manufacturers in various color ranges, some limited, others extensive. Rely on your needlework shop to recommend appropriate canvas and yarn combinations.

Knitting worsted is a tightly twisted 4-ply yarn whose fibers are shorter than tapestry or Persian yarns and hence less durable. It should not be used for rugs at all, but is a thrifty alternative in wall hangings where wearability is not a requisite. Use one thread on Number 10 canvas, double it for Number 7. It cannot be separated for finer canvas work.

Miscellaneous fibers, such as embroidery cottons, silks, metallic threads, raffia, and string, can provide decorative effects in wall hangings (they are not hardy enough for rug wear). They are usually applied over existing stitches but can be used alone if they cover the canvas adequately.

Yarn Requirement

To figure your yarn needs, you must first select your canvas, yarn, and the stitch or stitches you plan to use, since some require more yarn than others. Then on your 3-inch seam allowance or other scrap of canvas, work up an inch-square sample in each stitch; calculate the yarn needed for each sample by noting the length of yarn in your needle at the start and finish. By correlating the yarn needed per square inch with accurate measurements of the area of your project by color and by stitch, you will be able to figure your entire yarn needs. You can also call on your yarn supply shop to make this estimate for you.

Buy generous quantities of yarn to avoid even the slightest variation in dye lots; you may be able to return unused skeins or packages.

Needles

Needles for canvas work have dulled points and are available in various sizes. In general, use Number 13 or 14 needle on Number 5 canvas, Number 15 needle on Number 7 canvas, and Numbers 17, 18, or 19 needle on Number 10 canvas or finer. The needle should thread easily, but its eye should not be so big that it crowds the canvas threads during stitching.

Stitching

The five needlepoint stitches selected for this

book all meet certain requirements: historically, they are traditional rugmaking stitches; they duplicate, or at least simulate, the surface texture of period rugs, and they provide the characteristics necessary for a good rug stitch: tightness of weave to prevent snagging; good coverage; adequate underpadding; and minimal distortion. If you want to duplicate a looped or cut pile, use Turkey tufting, which authentically reproduces the Turkish knot and simulates the texture of the Persian and Spanish knots. If you want a flat-woven surface, choose among the remaining four stitches, each of which offers a different look. You can also combine stitches successfully in the same project.

Note: In the following stitch diagrams, start at the back of the canvas, and in sequence, come up at the odd numbers and down at the even numbers.

Basketweave. This stitch can be done on mono or penelope canvas. From the front it looks like its familiar sister stitches, the half cross and continental, but it is the only one of the three sufficiently lacking in distortion to be used for rugs or wall hangings.

Start the basketweave at the top right-hand corner of the design and follow the sequence of numbers (*see* Figure 3). You can see that the

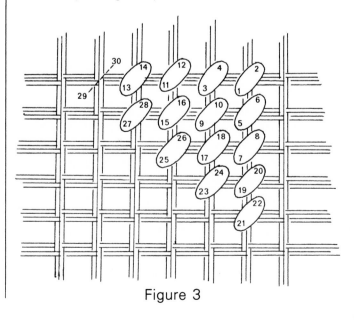

Figure 3

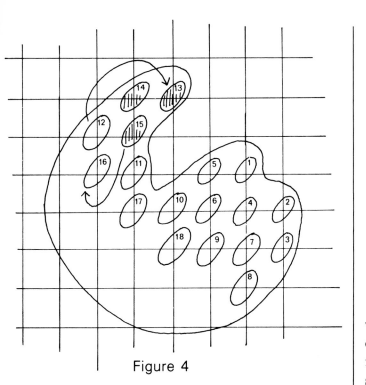

Figure 4

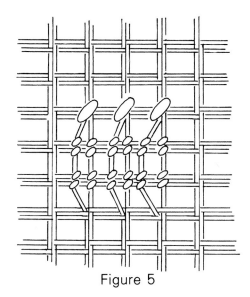

Figure 5

rows are worked diagonally. Be careful to alternate the direction of those diagonal rows—one up, the next down—because if two contiguous rows are stitched in the same direction, they will create a ridge.

If you have difficulty maintaining the basket-weave pattern within odd-shaped design areas, intersperse individual stitches as needed (*see* Figure 4). You can also turn the needlepoint canvas upside down to get to otherwise hard-to-reach areas. In this way sections that were formerly to the right and above your work area will now be accessible to the left and below it. The diagonal stitches will look identical, whether the canvas is right side up or upside down.

If you are using penelope canvas, you can divide each of the double-thread intersections (over which you would normally make one stitch) into four smaller single-thread intersections. Simply spread the double threads apart and stitch over the resulting four intersections with finer yarn (*see* Figure 5). In this way you can quadruple the number of stitches in a given area and incorporate more detailed motifs within a coarsely stitched background. This flexibility may very

well dictate your choice of penelope over mono canvas, especially if there are intricate designs or medallions within large areas of plain background.

Cross stitch. This must be done on penelope canvas where the double intersection locks the stitch. You can start a row of cross stitches at the right or left, and form the stitches either individually (*see* Figure 6 A) or in multiple (*see* Figure 6 B), working half the crosses all along one

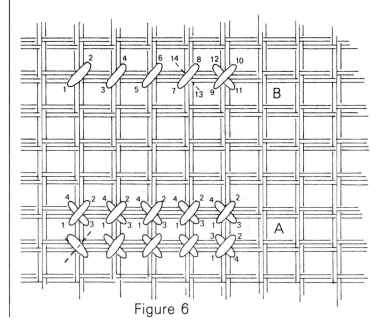

Figure 6

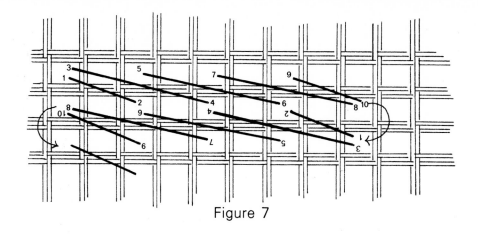

Figure 7

row, then returning on the same row to cross those diagonal arms. The latter method is quicker but provides less padding. Whichever way you form the cross stitch, remember to face all the top strokes in the same direction.

Since you must cross each intersection twice to form this stitch, you will find that in order not to crowd the canvas threads you will need to use lighter weight yarn for the cross stitch than you would use for other stitches on the same canvas.

Soumak stitch.   This stitch is named for the Soumak weave, one of the flat oriental weaves. Use either mono or penelope canvas and work from left to right (*see* Figure 7). When you reach the end of the row, turn the canvas upside down so you will still be working from left to right on the return row. The stitch covers the canvas quickly and works best with large-sized geometric motifs and designs.

Gobelin stitch.   Named after the French tapestry works, this simple vertical stitch covers best on mono canvas. It can be worked either from right to left or from left to right (*see* Figure 8), and while it is usually made over two horizontal threads, a finer version can be stitched over

one horizontal thread. For adequate canvas coverage, you may have to add an additional strand to the yarn you would ordinarily use for basketweave, Soumak or Turkey tufting on the same mesh canvas. For full coverage, be sure the yarn lays flat.

Turkey tufting.   Turkey tufting on penelope canvas is formed exactly like the rya knot on fabric and the Turkish knot on a loom. All three produce a looped stitch which can be cut into pile.

Always work Turkey tufting from the bottom of the canvas to the top, and from left to right.

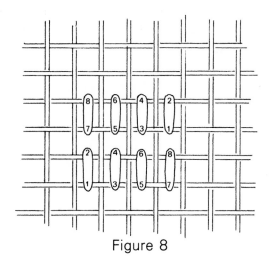

Figure 8

To make the first stitch (*see* Figure 9), insert your needle through the front of the canvas at A, pulling it through just until a tail of yarn remains in front exactly as long as you want the pile or loop to be. With your left hand, hold this tail of yarn down, and with your right hand, bring the needle up through the canvas at B, down at C, and up again at D (in the same hole where you began the stitch). Pull the yarn toward you to lock the loop.

Make the next stitch (*see* Figure 10) in exactly the same way as you made the first, except that instead of holding down a tail of yarn, you will hold down the loop at the arrow. Keep the loops uniform in size by hooking the yarn around a straight edge or your thumb. Continue to form stitches, and when you reach the end of the row, cut the yarn the same length as the loops. Start the next row at the left side, working in every

other row (*see* Figure 11). Cut the loops into pile every few rows.

You can see that Turkey tufting is normally worked in alternate rows. You can produce a denser pile by making the stitches in every row.

Joining

The least visible and most effective way of joining two or more sections of canvas is by the overlapping method. Briefly described, you simply overlap canvas in the areas to be joined and stitch through two or more layers of the mesh. While there are other ways to join two pieces of needlepoint—for example, by seaming them as you would any two pieces of fabric or by whipping them together—the overlapping method is the best way of joining any stitch, detailed design, and more than two sections of needlework.

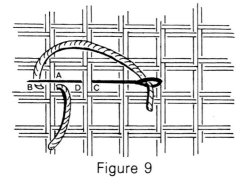

Figure 9

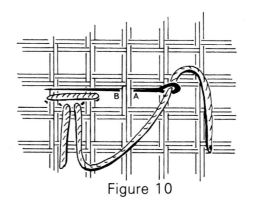

Figure 10

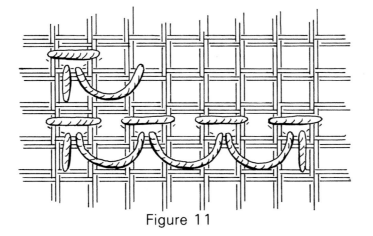

Figure 11

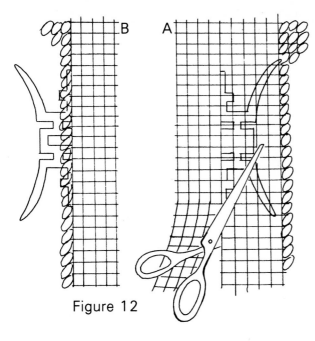

Figure 12

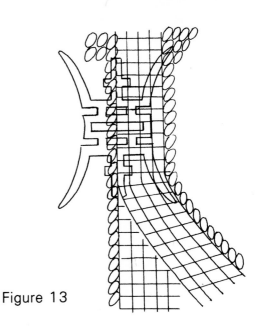

Figure 13

To make an overlapping join, first work up to within two inches of the pattern outline on both sections of canvas. Then, on the right piece, carefully cut the canvas just outside the pattern outline (*see* Figure 12 A) and on the left piece, count five extra canvas threads beyond the pattern outline and cut the canvas between the fifth and sixth threads (*see* Figure 12 B). To prevent unraveling of the outer threads, sparingly apply latex, colorless nail polish, or any white all-purpose glue to the cut canvas edges and let dry.

Lay the last five rows of the right piece over the first five rows of the left piece, matching the mesh and design exactly (*see* Figure 13). Carefully align the overlapped canvas, then whip the two pieces together with heavy thread (*see* Figure 14). Continue to needlepoint over the doubled canvas as if it were a single layer, following your design. The join may be made anywhere in the pattern, but try to place it in the middle of

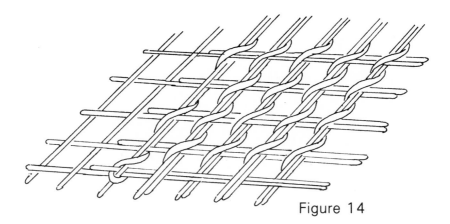

Figure 14

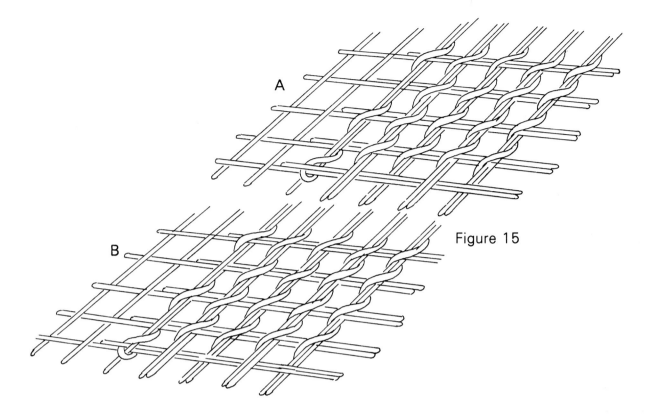

A

B

Figure 15

an intricate design, where the faint ridge will not be noticeable, rather than in a large single-color area or in the background.

To make a four-way join, first prepare two overlapping joins as described above. Then treating the two edges which will eventually be joined as above, cut the canvas on the top overlap just outside the pattern outline, and cut the canvas on the bottom section between the fifth and sixth unworked canvas threads. Bring the top overlap (*see* Figure 15 A) down over the bottom overlap (*see* Figure 15 B), matching the mesh and design motifs carefully. Align the overlapped canvas and tack the two sections together with heavy thread, anchoring some of the stitches. Continue to needlepoint over the multiple layers of canvas as if through a single layer. There will be four layers of canvas in the center, which will require care in stitching through the proper mesh. Obviously, the quadruple layer will be thicker than other parts of your work, so try to plan any four-way

joins in complex or many-colored areas of design where they will be less noticeable.

Blocking

Needlepoint rugs and wall hangings made in the basketweave, Soumak or cross stitches will probably have to be blocked because these slanting stitches tend to pull the canvas out of shape. Turkey tufting and Gobelin projects may not need blocking at all because those vertical stitches don't exert a distorting diagonal pull on the canvas. Whatever blocking needs to be done should follow the joining process.

For blocking use a large enough piece of wood to accommodate your joined canvas. You may need an old door, a full sheet of plywood, or even the attic floor to block a large project. Cover the blocking board with brown paper outlined with the finished size of the rug or hanging. Then place the needlepoint face down on the brown paper and tack the two upper corners with non-rusting tacks, matching the finished stitching with the outline (*see* Figure 16). Secure the tacks through the taped canvas edges.

Dampen the back of the stitched needlepoint by steaming it with an iron held a few inches above the canvas or by sponging the canvas with a wet cloth. When the needlepoint is sufficiently damp, you will be able to pull it into conformity with the outline on the brown paper. Stretching and pulling the canvas evenly on all sides, tack the third and fourth corners, and then tack the

entire perimeter at 1-inch intervals (*see* Figure 17). Leave the board in a horizontal position and let the needlepoint dry for two or three days.

If you don't think you can manage the blocking and joining yourself, take your needlepoint to a professional to finish. Upholsterers and even some furriers work with needlepoint, as well as the needlework shops. Professional work comes relatively high, but a needlepoint rug or hanging merits excellent care.

For additional information on finishing, see Chapter 21.

Figure 16   Figure 17

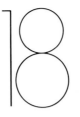

Latch Hooking

Backing Material

Latch hooking is done on coarsely woven rug canvas which can accommodate 3 or 4 stitches per linear inch (that is, 9 or 16 stitches per square inch). For a slightly denser pile, you can also hook on Number 5 penelope needlepoint canvas, which produces 25 stitches per square inch.

To prepare the canvas for work, cut it 4 inches wider and longer than your finished project in order to have a 2-inch seam allowance on all four sides. If you are making your rug in more than one section, provide for these 2-inch margins on all sections (*see below* for joining instructions). Bind all cut canvas edges with masking or fabric tape to prevent fraying.

Yarn

Various manufacturers offer precut hooking yarn. The yarns differ slightly in length and thickness, but in general they are about 2½ inches long and have 4 to 6 loosely twisted plies. Also available is a precut rya-type yarn which is a little longer and more tightly twisted and designed to simulate the look of authentic rya through latch hooking.

The range of colors available from any one manufacturer is rather limited. You can increase it either by using yarns from various suppliers or

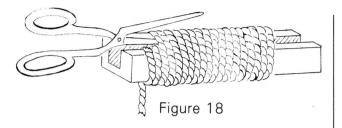
Figure 18

by cutting your own lengths from skeins of rug yarn of appropriate weight. Cut each piece at least 2½ inches long; if you want a higher pile, cut it as long as you wish, figuring that the knot of the stitch will itself require over half an inch. The easiest way to make evenly cut lengths for hooking is to use a commercial yarn gauge or to make your own by grooving a piece of wood of the proper perimeter (see Figure 18).

Precut yarn is commonly available in 1-ounce packs with 320 to 360 pieces. Sometimes the exact number is designated on the wrapper. Since one length of yarn is used for each stitch, you can easily determine how many packages of each color yarn you will need to cover your particular canvas.

Stitching

Latch hooking is done with a special tool which incorporates at the end of a metal shank a hook and a free-swinging bar, which when closed against the hook, creates in effect a needle's eye.

To make a stitch, fold a piece of yarn over the shank of the tool just under the latch bar. Insert the hook into one mesh of canvas and out the hole just above so that the shank is covered by one horizontal pair of threads (see Figure 19). The latch hook can face either right or left. Tuck both loose ends of yarn under the hook (see Figure 20). Hold the loose ends with one hand while you draw the hook toward you until the latch closes against the hook. Continue to pull the hook until the ends of the yarn have completely passed through the loop (see Figure 21). Finally, secure the knot by pulling the ends tight.

With the selvages of the rug canvas running up and down, work your rug or hanging from the bottom to the top so that each new knot falls over the previously stitched row below it. You can work either from right to left or from left to right on each row, making certain that you fill in every hole and that you always insert the latch hook in the same direction so the tails of every stitch point toward the bottom.

Joining

Sections of rug canvas are easily joined by overlapping them and hooking through the doubled canvas. However, the canvas mesh of both sections must run in the same direction; that is, the selvages on both pieces must run vertically.

First, work up to about the last inch within the

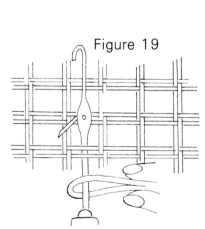
Figure 19

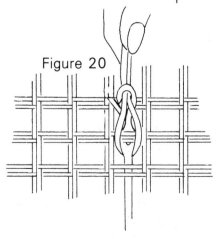
Figure 20

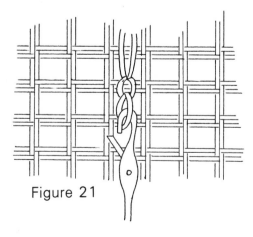
Figure 21

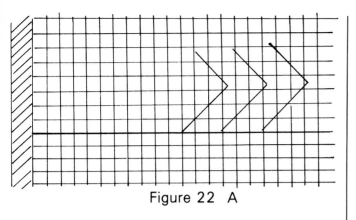

Figure 22   A

design on the sides to be joined. On the top section mark the limits of the design; add four extra meshes and cut between the fourth and fifth threads (*see* Figure 22 A). On the bottom piece mark the limits of the design and cut the

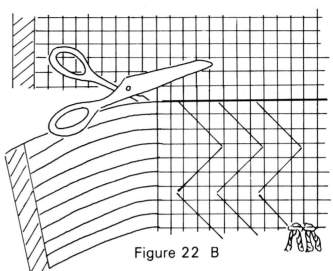

Figure 22   B

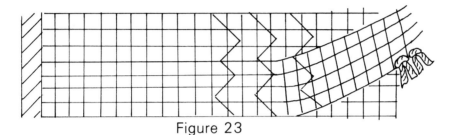

Figure 23

canvas carefully just outside this thread (*see* Figure 22 B).

To actually join the two pieces, lay the bottom section over the meshes of the top section so that the design on both top and bottom pieces just meets (*see* Figure 23). Carefully match the overlapped threads and secure the doubled canvas by basting over one intersection at a time (*see* Figure 24). Now hook through the doubled canvas

as if it were a single layer, following the design of your porject. The pile of the stitches will completely obscure the area of joining.

If you are joining sections of canvas vertically, follow the same procedures, but in this case overlap the sections from right to left rather than from bottom to top.

For information on finishing procedures, see Chapter 21.

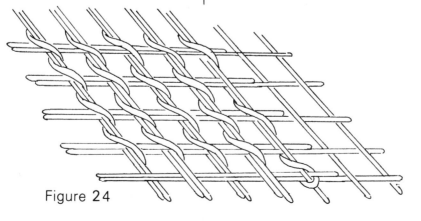

Figure 24

Rya

Backing Material

Imported rya backing is made of linen and wool. The weft threads are densely woven and the warp threads well spaced, about 6 to the inch. Every ½ inch a gap in the weft threads creates a row in which to make the stitches.

Imported Scandinavian backing comes by the yard in various widths, ranging from 17 to 27 inches, as well as in many special sizes already bound and finished. If this heavy-duty rya backing is not available, you can utilize any densely woven material by pulling out one or two weft (horizontal) threads every ½ inch to create the stitching row.

Try to select a backing in the width of your finished rug or hanging so the selvages will double as side hems; the long pile of the stitches will hide the selvages. Hem both ends so that no finishing tasks remain after the rug has been stitched. Simply turn the backing under two times, as you would a regular hem, then tack securely to the back. If you need to hem the sides, do so in the same way.

Yarn

Rya yarn is tightly twisted 2-ply wool that is sold by the skein in two weights and a large number of colors and shades. Cut the skein through only once so you will have long strands. When making rugs, use 3 strands of the heavier yarn; for wall hangings use 4 strands of the lighter yarn. Use a large Number 13 tapestry needle with both weights of wool.

Yarn requirements depend so heavily on the exact backing material, weight of the yarn, and especially the length of the pile, that you will have to rely on the estimate of the needlework shop where you buy the materials, or work up your own sample to determine exact amounts.

Stitching

The rya knot is formed like the loomed Turkish knot and like Turkey tufting on needlepoint canvas, but its loops are often left much longer, sometimes up to three inches for a rug. You can create special effects by varying the lengths of the loops and by leaving some of them uncut.

Start stitching in the bottom row of the backing at the left selvage (*see* Figure 25). To make one knot, insert your needle through the front at A, pulling it through until a tail of yarn remains in front just as long as you want the pile or loop to be. With your left hand hold this tail of yarn down, and with your right hand bring the needle up through the backing at B, down at C, and up again at D in the same slot in which you began the knot. You can see that one knot is looped around two warp threads.

Make the next knot (*see* Figure 26) in exactly the same way as you did the first, except instead of holding a tail of yarn, you will hold a loop. Keep the loops uniform by hooking them around a straight edge or your thumb. Always work across the row from left to right, and at the end of each row, cut the yarn the same length as the loop. Start again at the left selvage and work the next row immediately above the just-completed row. Cut the loops in a random, uneven manner every few rows; they should not look like neatly trimmed pile.

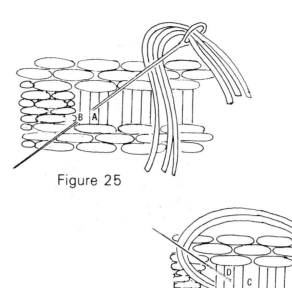

Figure 25

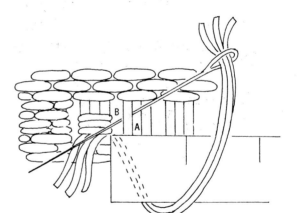

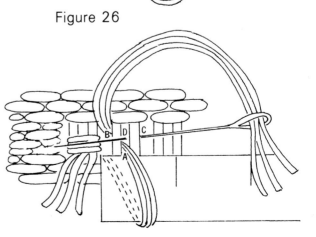

Figure 26

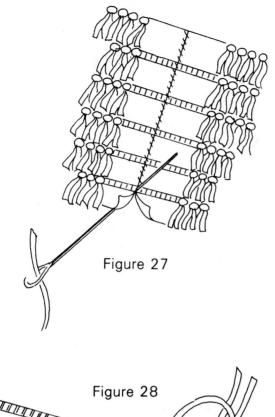

Figure 27

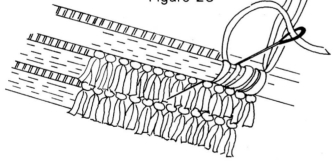

Figure 28

Joining

If you want to join two pieces of backing to make a wide rug, simply abut two selvage sides and whipstitch them together (*see* Figure 27). The seam will later be hidden by the long pile.

Fringing

If you want to fringe your rug, work the last stitching row at each end with extra long loops. At one end, the fringe will fall in the same direction as the stitching. At the other end, work the fringing row in the opposite direction with the loops facing out; mask the exposed backing with a blanket stitch (*see* Figure 28).

Fringing is not appropriate for wall hangings. See Chapter 21 for ways to mount and hang them.

20

Punch Hooking

Backing Material

Punch hooking is done on a densely woven cotton or linen material like cotton duck, warp cloth, monk's cloth, hopsacking, and Duraback. The fabric must be tightly enough woven to grip and retain each stitch, yet not so dense that you cannot push the punching needle into it fairly easily. The best backings have 12 to 15 warp and weft threads per inch and are suitable for heavy rug yarns and lighter worsteds. They are sold by the yard in widths up to about 200 inches.

Cut the backing at least 4 inches wider all around than your design in order to tack it to a frame for punching. Even if the design is round or oval, cut the backing material in a square or rectangle so it can be mounted on a punching frame.

Frame

In order to provide the surface tension needed to push the punching tool through the backing, the material must be tightly stretched over a frame. The frame can encompass the entire project, or it can be smaller than the finished rug or hanging, since the backing can be moved around on the frame and retacked, even through completed stitching, whenever you want to work in

169

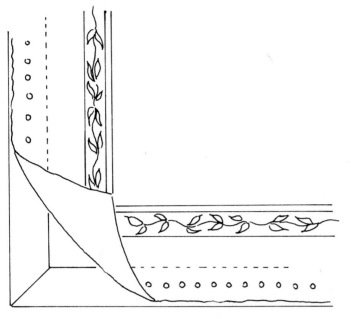

Figure 29

Yarn

Any material that passes easily through the eye of a punching needle and is durable enough for the use it will receive can be used for punch hooking. Rug wool, which is available in various weights, is highly recommended for floor coverings. The possibilities are greater for wall hangings: tapestry yarn, knitting worsted, synthetic fibers, even woven fabrics, nylon, leather, and plastic cut into thin strips. (Not all materials can be used in all the punching tools, nor are they equally effective on all backings.)

Before ordering your yarn, stitch a few inch-square samples in the hem of your backing fabric in different kinds of fibers and heights of loops. This way you will be able to determine whether you want to use heavier yarn with fewer stitches per square inch, or lighter weight yarn with denser loops, and what height pile is most pleasing.

Since yarn requirements depend entirely on the weight of the yarn, the height of the loop and the closeness of the stitching, your best yarn estimate will come from the inch-square sample in the preferred wool and density. Simply pull out that yarn and measure it, then compute the amounts you need for the entire project.

Note: It is easier to work with free-pulling balls of yarn, so if your wool doesn't come in a pull skein, rewind it.

a different area of the project. To avoid constant retacking, use a frame that is at least 24 inches square or 20 by 36 inches.

Many kinds of frames are available commercially which are mounted on legs and adjust to various heights and dimensions. You can also make your own frame by assembling two pairs of artist's stretchers or by recycling a discarded picture frame of adequate size and strength.

To mount the backing, lay the fabric design-side up on the frame. Place the outer limits of the design at least an inch inside the frame so you have enough clearance for the punching needle. Secure the backing to the frame with tacks, a staple gun, or push pins, making sure that the fabric lies absolutely straight (see Figure 29).

During punching, the weight of the wool or the pressure of the stitching may loosen the tension on the backing, so you may have to retack it occasionally. Whenever you have to secure your project through already completed work, try to place the tacks between the stitches rather than through them.

Punching Tools

There are various devices available for punch hooking. The shuttle hooker "walks" automatically from stitch to stitch as its two-piece handle is shuttled back and forth. Its two needles accommodate either yarn or strips of fabric and make loops from ¼-inch to 1 inch high.

The "egg beater" hooker also moves automatically from stitch to stitch as you turn the handle, making up to 500 uniform loops a minute in any of three heights. It is by far the fastest hooker, but its single needle takes only 4-ply knitting worsted, not heavy rug yarn.

The hand punch needle, readily available and inexpensive, is the most popular punching tool. It has a tubular needle at one end of the handle and a yarn carrier at the other end. More versatile models have interchangeable needles for heavy and light yarns and a stitching gauge with which to regulate the height of the loop from ¼-inch to 1 inch.

Instructions for threading and operating each punching tool are furnished with the device. The general stitching instructions which follow apply to all of them, although the drawings illustrate the punch needle.

Stitching

If you are using a frame without legs or a stand, rest it on your lap and against a table with the pattern facing you. This is actually the back of the rug or hanging since the design is punched from the back with the finished loop surface emerging on the underside.

When you thread the needle, be sure the yarn moves freely through the eye; any tug on it will make the loops uneven. To form the first loop, pull 2 inches of yarn through the eye. With one hand, hold the needle upright, and with the other, anchor the 2-inch tail of yarn on top of the backing. Push the needle through the backing (*see* Figure 30) until the handle reaches the surface of the fabric. Then pull the needle up just until it clears the surface of the fabric and, without raising it, slide it along to the point of your next stitch, keeping the yarn channel of the needle facing the direction in which you are stitching (*see* Figure 31). Continue stitching in this manner, swiveling the needle whenever you want to change the direction of stitching.

The closeness of the stitching depends on the weight of the yarn and the height of the loop. The thinner the yarn and the shorter the loop,

the closer together the stitches and rows should be. With a heavy rug yarn, a good guide is 24 to 30 stitches per inch in 4 or 5 rows of 6 stitches each. You can draw your own stitching lines on

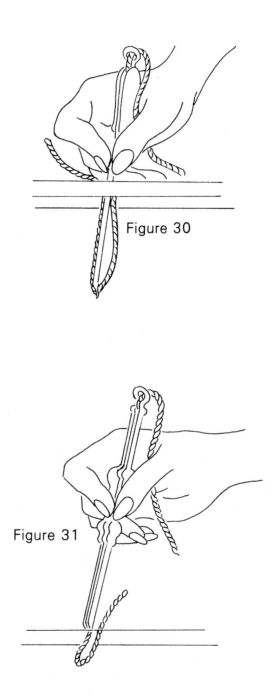

Figure 30

Figure 31

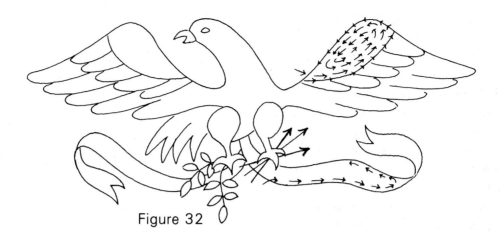

Figure 32

the backing about ¼-inch apart (*see* Figure 32). In all your work be sure the stitches are close enough together to cover the backing well but not so crowded that they pucker the project.

You can stitch the pattern in any sequence, but it is common to hook the smaller design areas surrounding the motifs (*see* Figure 33).

The background stitching can follow various patterns, depending on the effect you are striving for (*see* Figure 34). Straight lines give an angular, clean look to the background. Wavy lines in a random configuration allow the ground to recede.

Figure 33

first, then the borders, and last the background. First outline your design in a continuous row of punch hooking. Then, following the contours of that outline, stitch toward the center until the entire motif is filled in (*see* Figure 32). When you have completed an area or want to change colors, hold the last loop on the underside with one hand, and with the other, withdraw the needle entirely. Now you can cut the yarn without pulling any loops out. If you see that you will run out of yarn before you have finished a given area, just continue stitching until the yarn end passes through the yarn guide and then through the needle's eye. Then rethread the needle and continue stitching.

To give a motif or design area added importance, you can set it off with a little extra space around it, you can outline it in shorter loops, or you can actually shear and bevel the background

Figure 34

Swirls and circles emphasize the ground and give it motion and vigor. If you want to blend contiguous areas of color, stitch the common boundary in a jagged line (*see* Figure 35).

Note: Because you work from the back and the design emerges in a mirror image on the underside, remember to work all numbers and letters in reverse.

Joining

Since backing material is available in widths up to 200 inches, you should be able to make your rug in one piece. If for any reason you do need to join two sections, seam them together as you would two pieces of fabric. On both sections punch hook the design right up to the seaming edge. Then, with looped sides together and pattern matched, baste and then machine stitch the two pieces. Try to put your seam as close as you can to the hooking so the loops will hide the seam.

Latexing the Back

The back of a punch hooked rug or hanging—that is, the side facing you as you work—must be latexed to prevent the loops from pulling out. This can be done on the frame or not. Apply the liquid latex with a wide brush or spatula, spreading it evenly over the back of the stitching. For added protection to rugs, lay a piece of rug canvas over the backing before you apply the latex.

After the gummy substance has dried (in about a day), trim the unstitched backing fabric to within two inches of the finished hooking on all sides. At this point you can miter the corners and sew the hem to the backing (*see* Chapter 21). Or you can actually latex the hem to the backing by mitering the corners, folding the hem back on all sides, and pinning it securely to the backing. This is a particularly good way to finish curved pieces where you can pleat and then pin the hem. Apply

latex to the pinned hem and remove the pins when it has dried.

For additional information on finishing procedures, see Chapter 21.

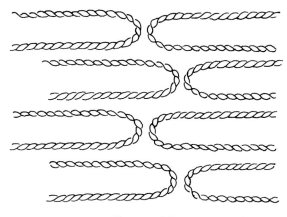

Figure 35

Finishing Touches

With the exception of rya projects, which are ordinarily knotted on prefinished backing, all rugs and wall hangings need some additional finishing touches. These might include hemming, binding, and some sort of fringing or edging, if desired. Lining, however, is not recommended because dust and dirt easily collect between the lining and stitching.

Hemming

The same procedure is used for hemming and mitering the corners of rugs and wall hangings, whether they are in needlepoint, latch, or punch hooking.

First cut away any excess backing material on all sides to within 2 inches of the finished piece. Then trim each corner diagonally to within 1 inch of the stitching (*see* Figure 36 A). Apply a thin coating of latex or white, all-purpose glue to each cut edge and let dry.

At each corner, turn in the diagonal side (*see* Figure 36 B), then flap the adjoining sides over it (*see* Figure 36 C) and whip the adjoining hems into a mitered corner (*see* Figure 36 D). Be sure that no backing material is visible from the front, even if the outermost stitching is slightly pulled into the hem. Tack the hem unobtrusively to the back of the stitching.

174

Binding

Rug binding is not necessary, although needle-point, latch, and punch hooked rugs will benefit from its added protection. You apply the binding and hem the rug in the same operation.

Use 1½-inch-wide rug binding of sufficient length to cover the perimeter of your rug. Cut away any excess backing material on all sides to within 1¼ inches of the finished stitching. Now trim the four corners diagonally to within 1 inch of the stitching (*see* Figure 37). Place the rug face up and lay the binding along the excess backing, as close as you can to the rug stitching (*see* Figure 38), pinning the binding strip in place. Continue to frame the finished rug with the binding, turning the corners, until all the binding is in place and pinned. Join or overlap the two binding ends where they meet. Leave enough slack in the binding, particularly as you turn the corners, so the rug will not pucker or pull. Sew the binding to the hem allowance, as close as you can to the finished stitching.

Turn the rug face down and bring the rug binding toward the back. This will also fold the hem allowance under the binding at the same time so you can tack them both down to the back of the stitching (*see* Figure 39). As you turn the corners, tuck in the excess rug binding to form a miter.

Fringe

Rugs and hangings usually need no further adornment, but you may prefer to add an edging. Tassels, commercial fringe and elaborate finishings are available, but the classic edging is a knotted wool fringe at the two ends, originally derived from the way in which early weavers finished off the warp threads on their looms. Use one or more of the colors in your rug.

To make the fringe, cut yarn into lengths of 6 or more inches, depending on how long you want the fringe. Remember that the fringe will be less

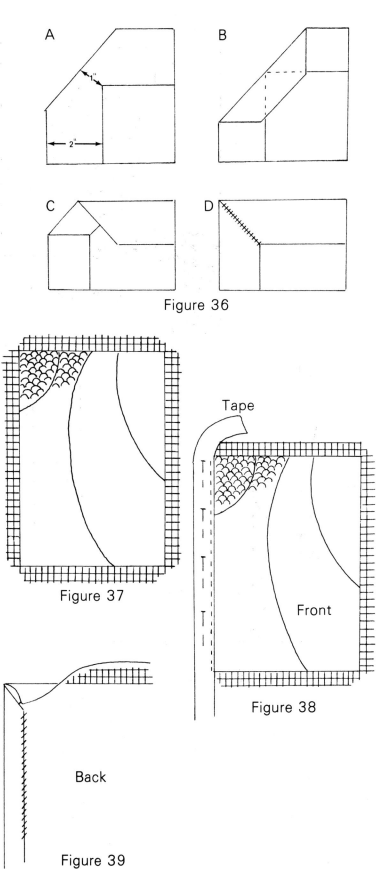

Figure 36

Figure 37

Figure 38

Figure 39

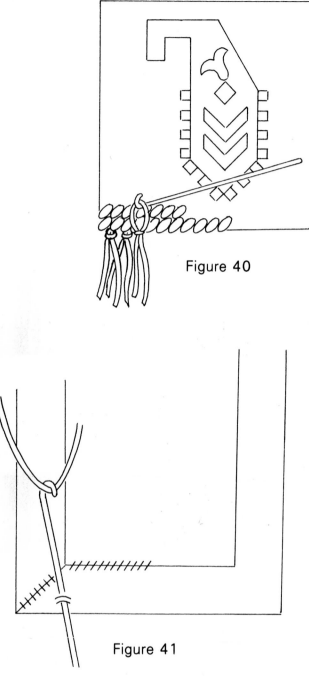

Figure 40

than half the length of the yarn piece. To insert the fringe into latch or needlepoint canvas, put a crochet needle into the last unworked row of canvas or even between finished stitches. Fold the yarn over the hook of the crochet needle and pull a small loop through the mesh (*see* Figure 40). Slip the two ends of the yarn through the loop, then pull them tight to secure the knot. If you want a thicker fringe, use thicker yarn or make two loops through each mesh. If you are fringing all around, be sure to insert extra loops through the corner mesh.

If you want to fringe a hooked rug which has been punched on a tightly woven backing, insert a small, sharp crochet needle just inside the hemmed edge (*see* Figure 41), then follow the fringing instructions above. If the material is too tightly woven to penetrate with the crochet needle, you will have to make a series of loops or blanket stitches at the bottom of the hem to anchor the fringe (*see* Figure 42).

Figure 41

Figure 42

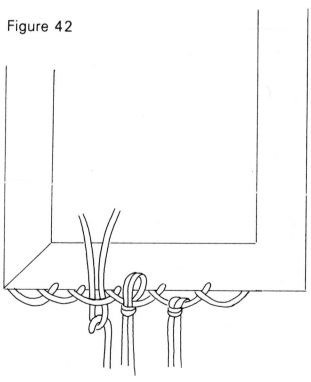

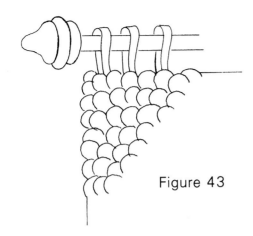

Figure 43

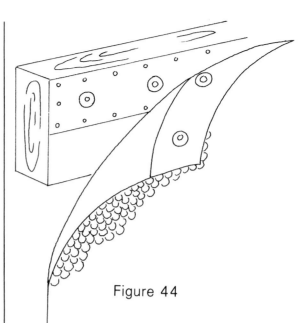

Figure 44

Mounting

Wall hangings and rugs can be displayed on the wall in various ways, but they are never framed. You can mount them on decorative wooden or metal curtain rods with rings or loops (*see* Figure 43).

You can blind mount the hanging on a strip of wood by means of upholstery grippers. Tack one strip of the gripper tape to a strip of wood and sew its mate to the top of the hanging (*see* Figure 44). Mount the wooden strip on the wall. You can easily unfasten the hanging for cleaning.

Care and Cleaning

An underpadding will help protect your rug from excessive wear and prolong its life. Vacuum it regularly so dirt does not penetrate and lodge in the stitches, and have it dry cleaned periodically, just as you would any other wool rug. Wall hangings need no special care other than an occasional vacuuming.

III

A
Portfolio
of
Design
Adaptations
for
Rugs
and
Wall
Hangings

Persian—Kashan

TYPICAL COLOR SCHEME	ALTERNATE I	ALTERNATE II
ivory	white	apricot
red	pink	beige
green	light green	orange
gold	hot pink	olive green
medium blue	yellow	pale green
deep blue	dark green	rust
navy	brown	black

180

Persian—Khorassan

TYPICAL COLOR SCHEME	ALTERNATE I	ALTERNATE II
ivory	pale yellow	pale pink
light blue	light blue	pink
green gold	blue	gold
orange	medium green	beige
medium blue	dark green	turquoise
navy	brown	navy

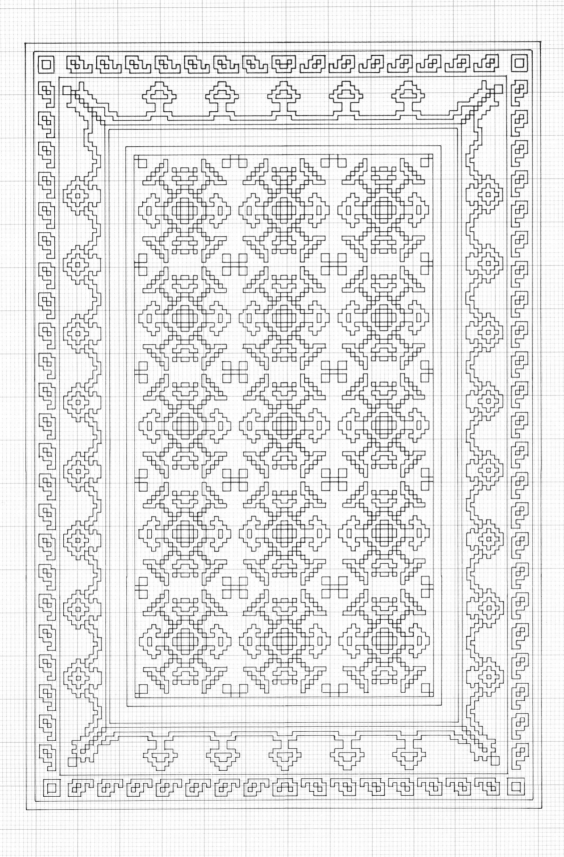

Persian—Kirman

TYPICAL COLOR SCHEME	ALTERNATE I	ALTERNATE II
ivory	pale yellow	pale blue
gold	orange	rose
light blue	light green	turquoise
red	deep green	deep blue
deep blue	gold	lavender
navy	brown	navy

184

Persian—Sarouk

TYPICAL COLOR SCHEME	ALTERNATE I	ALTERNATE II
ivory	pale yellow	white
red orange	pink	pale blue
olive green	olive green	rust
deep blue	medium brown	orange
red brown	dark brown	brown

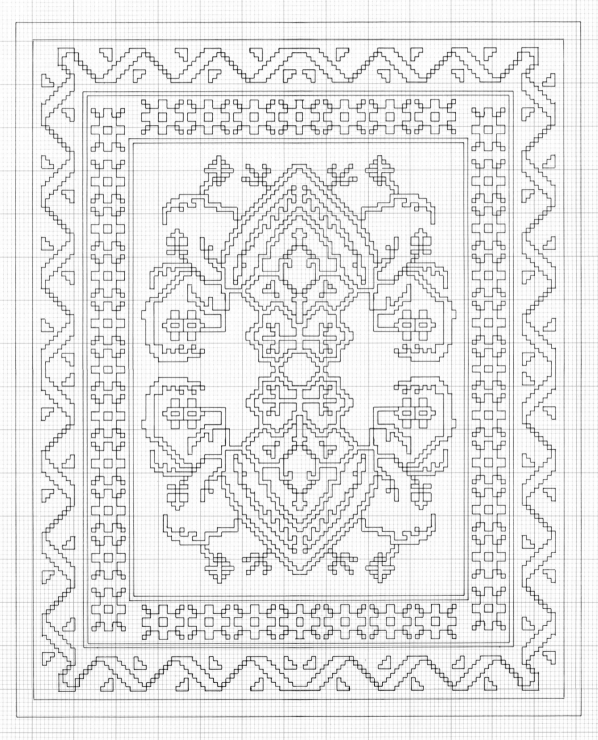

Indian

TYPICAL
COLOR
SCHEME

	ALTERNATE I	ALTERNATE II
dark blue	dark gray	deep brown
medium blue	taupe	turquoise
red	orange	beige
green	yellow	dark green
pink	lavender	light green
gold	light green	yellow
ivory	pale yellow	rose

188

Turkish—Ladik

TYPICAL COLOR SCHEME	ALTERNATE I	ALTERNATE II
ivory	pale yellow	white
light blue	orange	light green
dull red	medium brown	medium blue
olive green	rust	deep rose
navy	dark brown	dark green

190

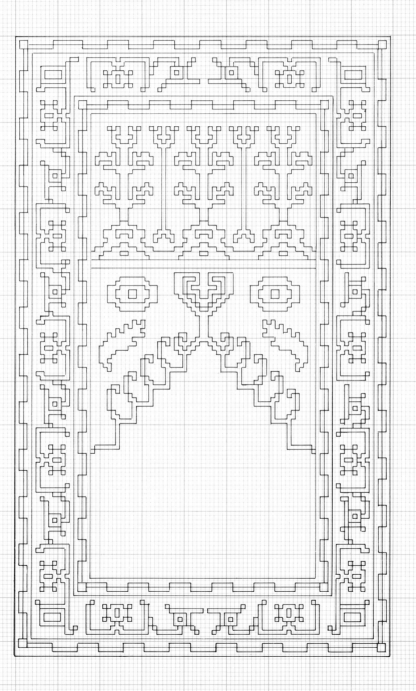

Caucasian—Kazak

**TYPICAL
COLOR
SCHEME**　　**ALTERNATE I**　　**ALTERNATE II**

white	yellow	white
light gold	aqua	pale yellow
light blue	turquoise	yellow
gold	lavender	light green
red	pink	blue
turquoise	hot pink	royal blue
deep blue	brown	deep green

192

Turkoman—Bokhara

TYPICAL COLOR SCHEME	ALTERNATE I	ALTERNATE II
yellow	ivory	ivory
red orange	pale green	rose
red	green	lavender
red brown	blue	blue
black	navy	navy

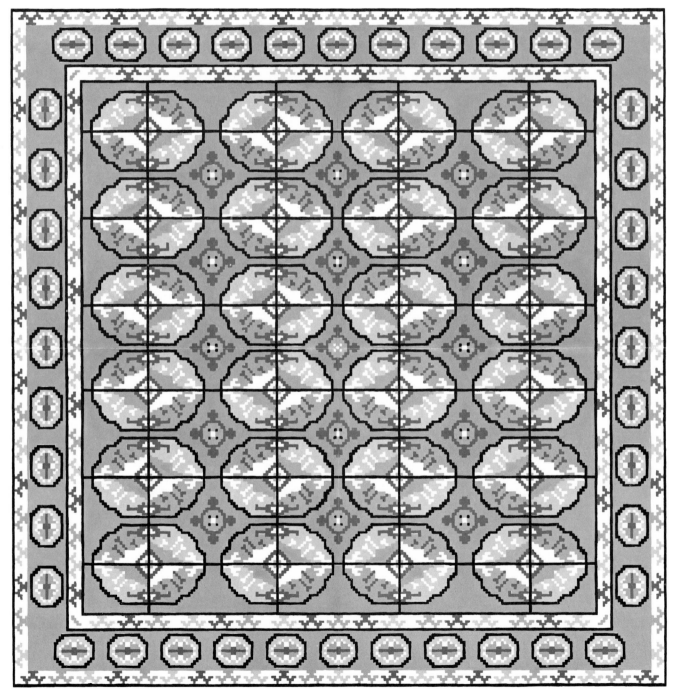

194

Samarkand

TYPICAL COLOR SCHEME	ALTERNATE I	ALTERNATE II
gold	aqua	white
red orange	pink	orange
turquoise	gold	yellow
medium blue	olive green	hot pink
deep royal blue	brown	black

196

Chinese

198

Chinese

TYPICAL COLOR SCHEME	ALTERNATE I	ALTERNATE II
pale blue	ivory	pale gold
pale gold	pale pink	pale blue
gold	pink	blue
burnt orange	light green	hot pink
medium blue	medium green	pink
deep blue	light brown	gray
navy	dark brown	charcoal

200

Spanish—Alcaraz

TYPICAL COLOR SCHEME	ALTERNATE I	ALTERNATE II
white	yellow	white
pale yellow	light green	pink
olive green	light blue	red
deep yellow	pink	deep ochre
burnt orange	hot pink	gold
royal blue	brown	navy

Spanish—Alpujarra

204

French—Louis XVI

206

French—19th Century	TYPICAL COLOR SCHEME	ALTERNATE I	ALTERNATE II
CENTER FIELD:			
background	pale gold	pale beige	light blue
cornucopia	deep gold with blue trim	deep orange with brown trim	light gold with blue trim
leaves in cornucopia	2 shades green	2 shades gold	2 shades green
fruit	orange; red; purple grapes	orange; red; green grapes	orange; red; green grapes
scrollwork	2 shades deep & royal blue	2 shades green	2 shades gold
roses	3 shades pink	3 shades coral	3 shades pink
leaves on roses	medium green	medium green	medium green
rosettes in field	red with light blue centers	orange with brown centers	ivory with light blue centers
FLORAL BORDER:			
roses	3 shades pink	3 shades pink	3 shades pink
scrollwork	2 shades light blue	2 shades green	2 shades gold
leaves	medium green	medium gold	medium green
background	very deep blue	medium brown	medium blue
INSIDE BAND:	deep gold	deep olive green	gold
NARROW SOLID BAND	pale gold	pale green	light blue
OAK LEAF BORDER:			
leaves	4 shades green	4 shades gold	4 shades green
acorns	2 shades red	2 shades brown	2 shades lavender
ribbons	red	olive green	blue
bow	2 shades red	2 shades brown	2 shades lavender
leaves at ribbon	medium green	medium gold	medium blue
background of ribbon	deep gold	deep olive green	gold
OUTSIDE BAND	royal blue	brown	navy

**TYPICAL
COLOR
SCHEME**

	TYPICAL COLOR SCHEME	ALTERNATE I	ALTERNATE II
	white	yellow	pink
	pale beige	light green	light gray
	beige	green	gray
	rose	lavender	pale yellow
	blue	pink	hot pink
	green	brown	deep gold

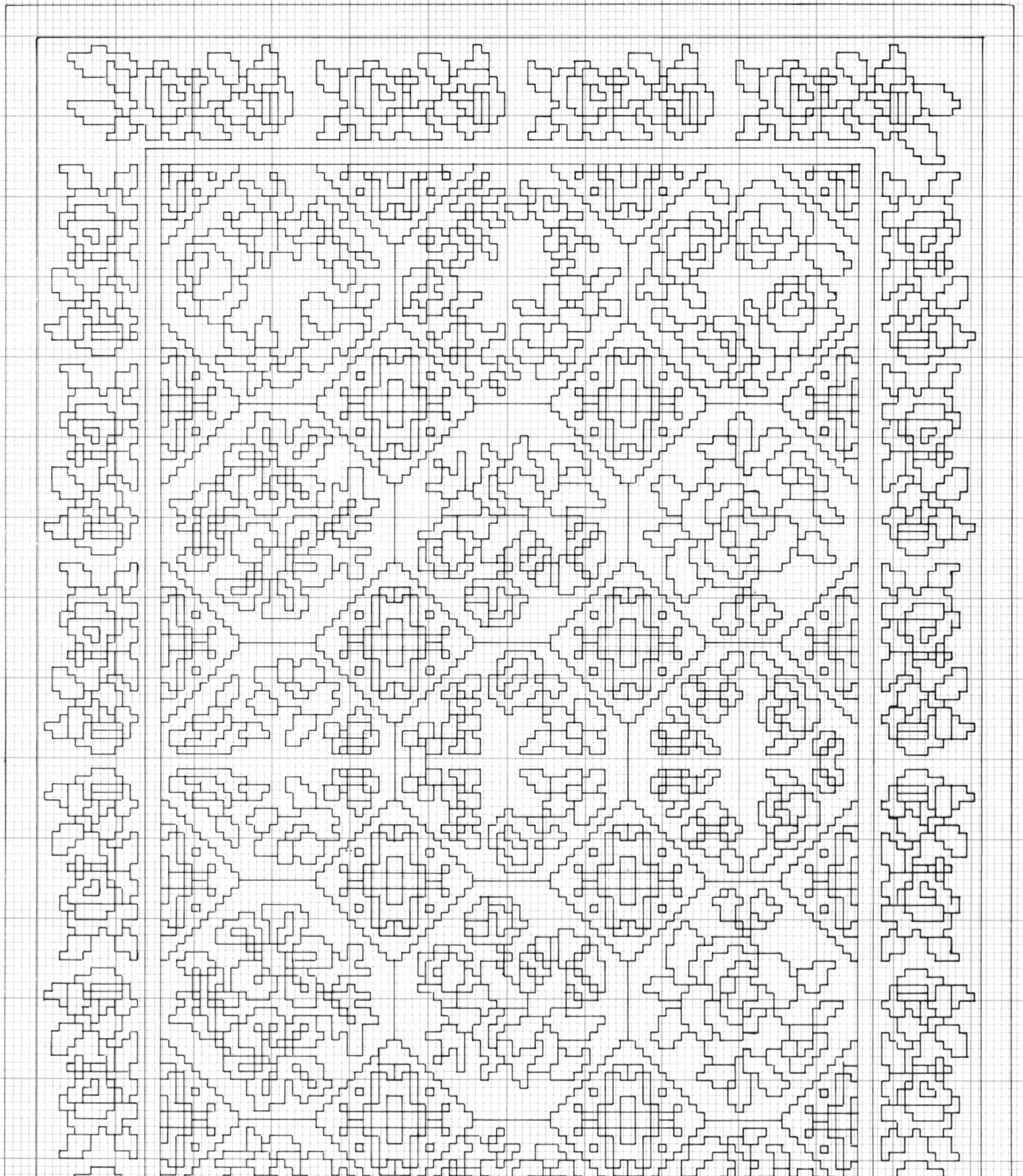

English	TYPICAL COLOR SCHEME	ALTERNATE I	ALTERNATE II
FLORAL CENTER FIELD: background	light green	beige	white
lilies	2 shades red with yellow & white centers	2 shades gold with pink & white centers	2 shades aqua with yellow & white centers
roses	3 shades: light to deep pink	3 shades red	3 shades gold
mallows	pale gold with deeper gold accents; deep pink centers	pale pink with deeper pink accents; red centers	pale blue with deeper blue accents; gold centers
small flowers	white; gold accents; red centers	white; gold accents; red centers	white; gold accents; aqua centers
leaves	dark green and medium green	dark & medium olive green	dark & medium blue green
INSIDE BAND	gold	gold	light blue
FLORAL BORDER: background	dark green	dark brown	navy
leaves	medium green with dark green veins	greens	greens
lilies	2 shades red with yellow & red centers	2 shades gold with pink & white centers	2 shades aqua with yellow & white centers
roses	2 shades pink with gold centers	2 shades red with gold centers	2 shades gold with aqua centers
small flowers	white; gold in middle; red in center	white; pink middle; red center	white; gold middle; ochre center
buds	light green	light green	light green
OUTSIDE BAND	light green	beige	light blue

212

Scandinavian

American Indian—Navajo, Chief Pattern

TYPICAL COLOR SCHEME	ALTERNATE I	ALTERNATE II
off white	pale blue	pale yellow
beige	lavender	yellow orange
taupe	light green	orange
rust	deep green	pink
medium brown	deep blue	hot pink
charcoal brown	navy	deep olive green

TYPICAL COLOR SCHEME	ALTERNATE I	ALTERNATE II
white	yellow	white
beige	pale green	pale blue
deep gold	orange	red
brick	rust	deep blue
royal blue	dark green	gold
black	brown	navy

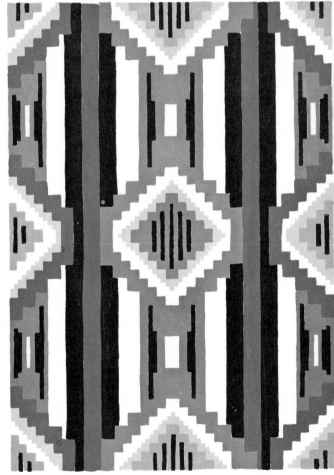

214

American Indian—Navajo, Serape Style

TYPICAL COLOR SCHEME	ALTERNATE I	ALTERNATE II
white	white	yellow
red	beige	green
blue	gold	beige
pink	red	medium brown
navy	black	dark brown

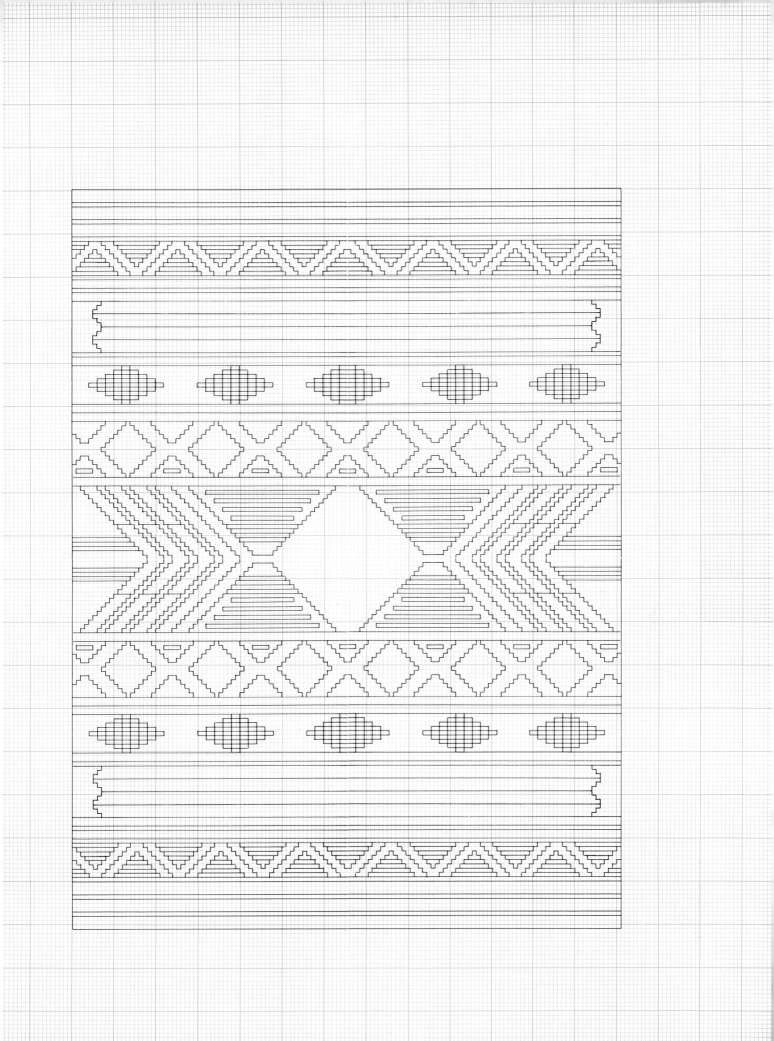

American Indian—Navajo, Two Gray Hills

TYPICAL COLOR SCHEME	ALTERNATE I	ALTERNATE II
white	white	pale yellow
beige	light blue	light green
burnt orange	blue	gold
red brown	light green	yellow ochre
brown	green	burnt orange
black	navy	dark brown

American Indian—Navajo, Yei Design

**TYPICAL
COLOR
SCHEME**

	TYPICAL COLOR SCHEME	ALTERNATE I	ALTERNATE II
	natural	pale yellow	white
	yellow	light green	light blue
	light brown	green	red
	deep brown	rust	blue
	orange	beige	aqua
	rust	medium brown	deep blue
	black	brown	navy

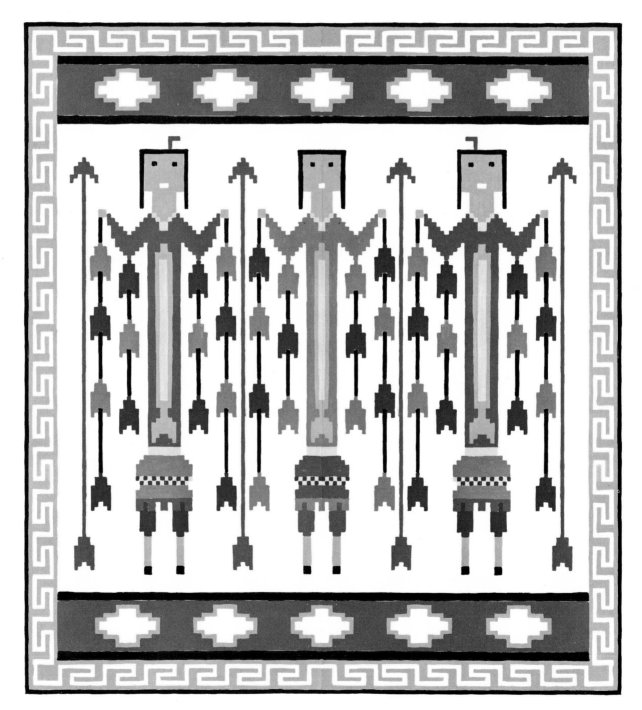

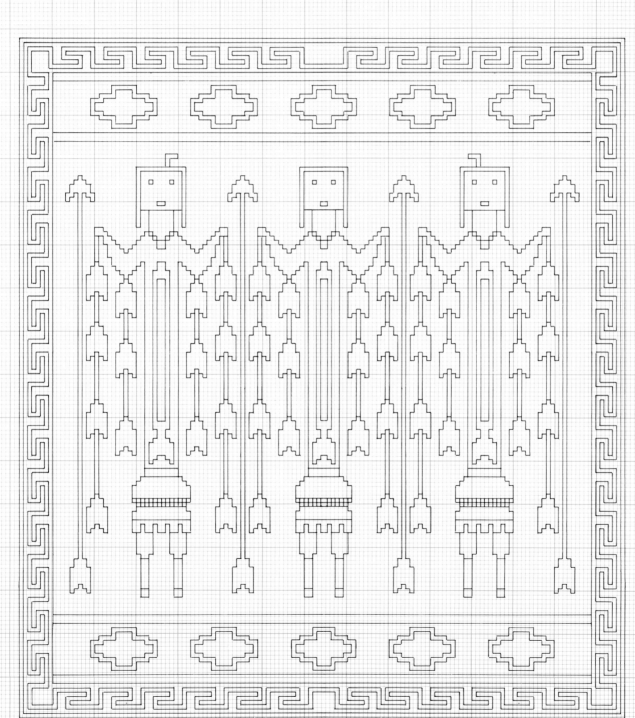

Early American

TYPICAL COLOR SCHEME	ALTERNATE I	ALTERNATE II
white	white	pale yellow
pale green	light blue	orange
yellow	lavender	light red
orange	deep lavender	deep red
light rose	aqua	beige
deep green	green	green
deep rose	turquoise	brown

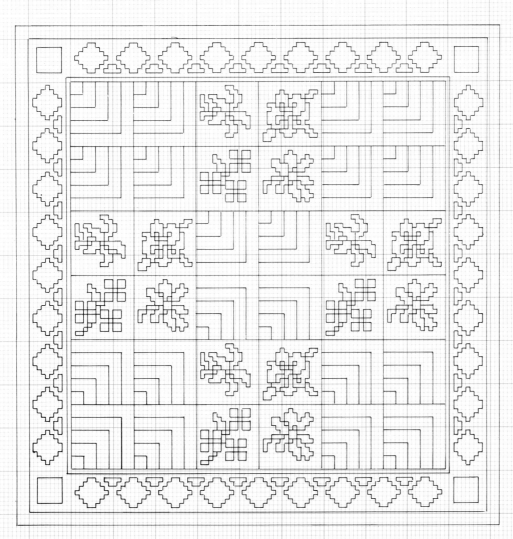

Early American

TYPICAL COLOR SCHEME	ALTERNATE I	ALTERNATE II
gold	light blue	light green
pink	aqua	apricot
light red	turquoise	orange
red	teal blue	burnt orange
light green	light green	light ochre
deep green	green	deep ochre
black	brown	dark green

Early American

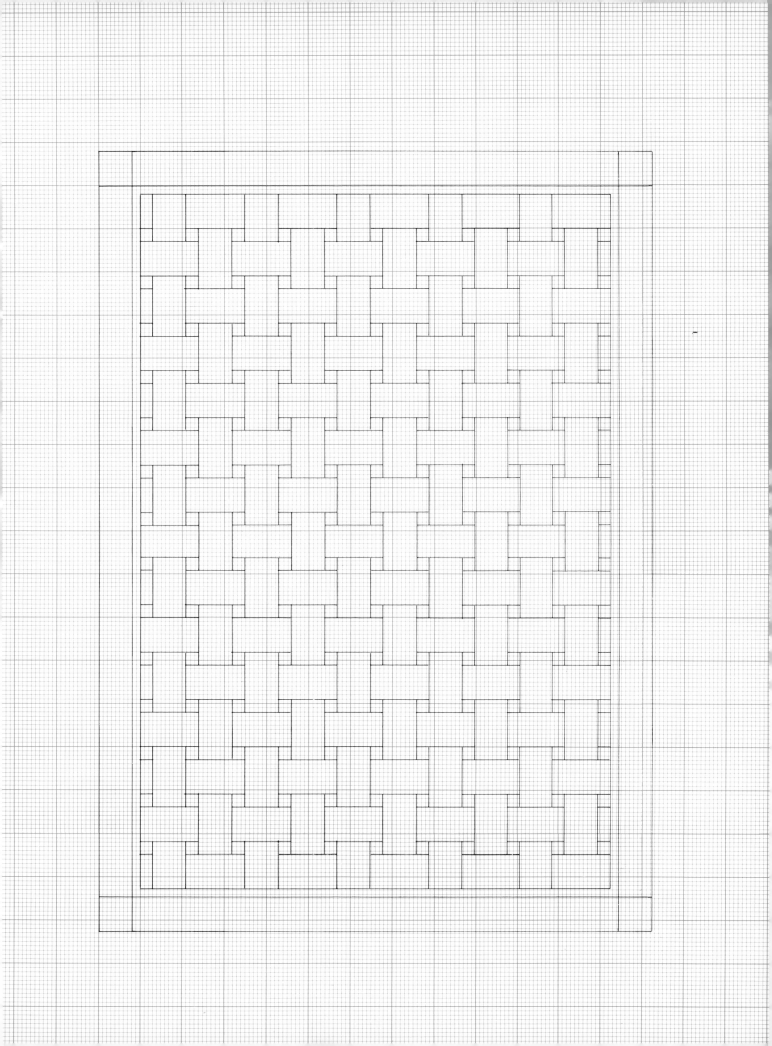

Contemporary American

SCHEME I	SCHEME II	SCHEME III
beige	white	aqua
gold	light green	kelly green
copper	royal blue	royal blue
brown	navy	brown

Contemporary American

SCHEME I	SCHEME II	SCHEME III
white	orange	beige
lemon yellow	red	brown
light blue	yellow	light green
kelly green	hot pink	gold
navy	navy	dark green

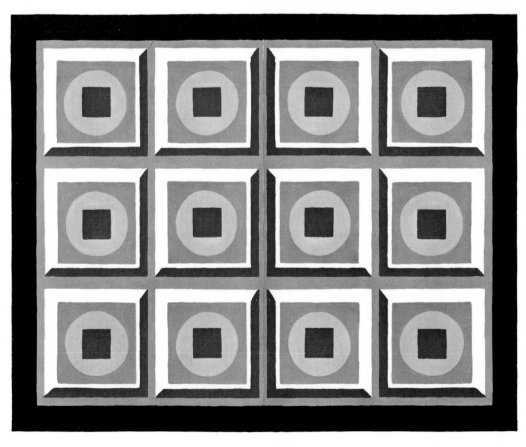

228

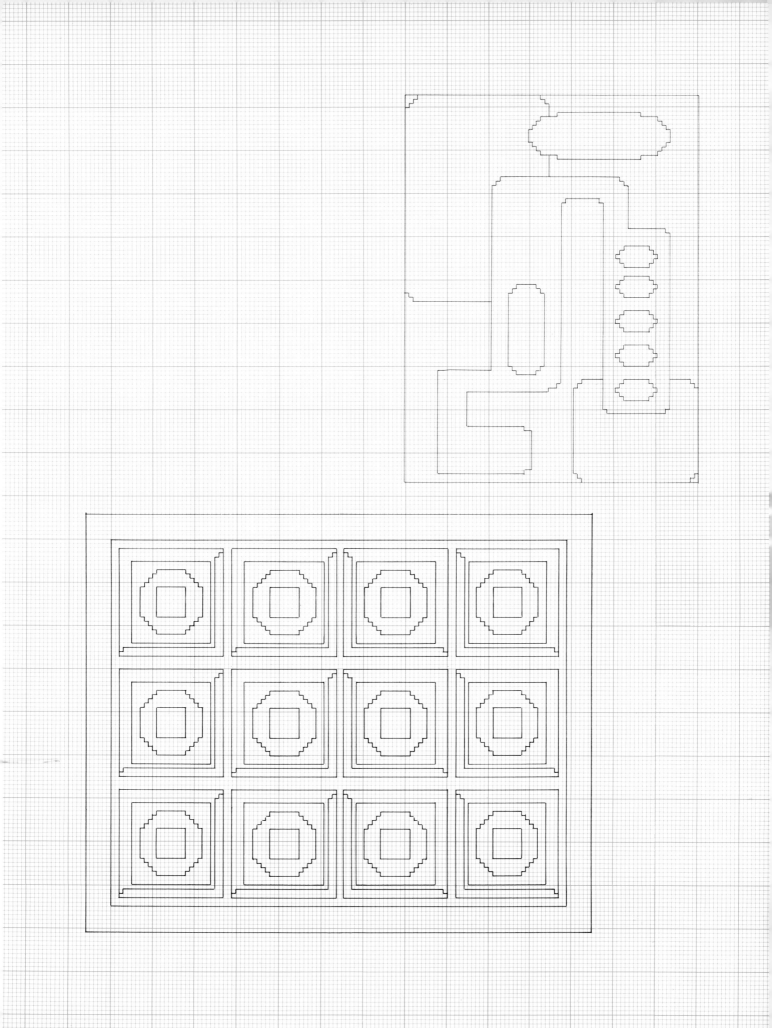

Contemporary American

SCHEME I	SCHEME II	SCHEME III
white	light blue	pale pink
yellow	pale green	gold
pink	kelly green	beige
orange	navy	brown

Contemporary American

SCHEME I	SCHEME II	SCHEME III
white	yellow	pale green
red	orange	gold
black	brown	navy

230

Contemporary American

SCHEME I	SCHEME II	SCHEME III
white	white	pale yellow
lemon yellow	aqua	yellow
yellow	turquoise	yellow orange
yellow orange	teal blue	orange
orange	medium blue	red orange
red orange	blue	red
red	navy	black

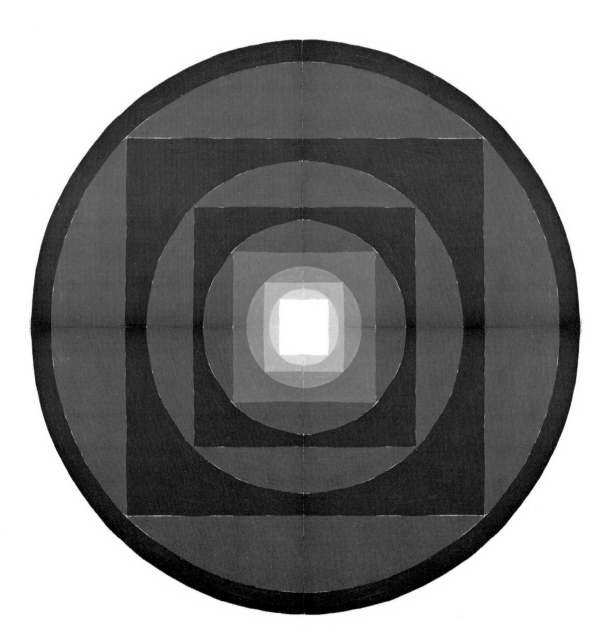

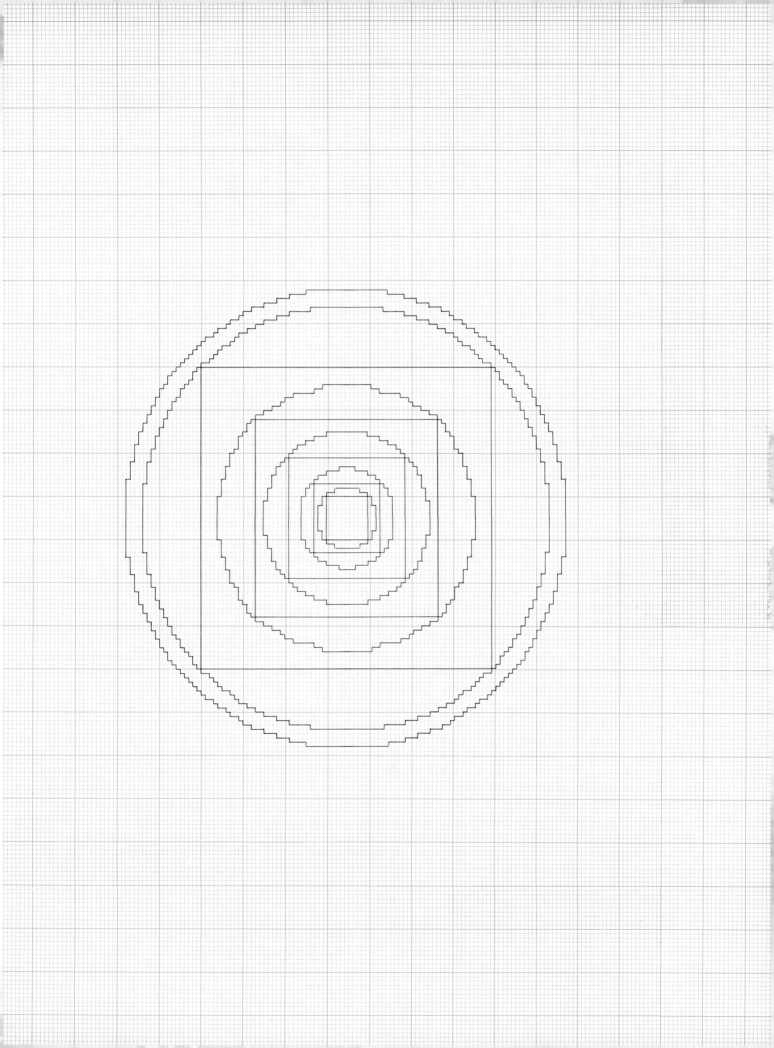

Sources of Supplies

The following retail sources carry different rug-making supplies. Some of them will send catalogs, brochures, and yarn samples. Contact them for current information.

Berit's Broidery, P.O. Box B, Bethesda, Maryland 20014. Rya.

Black Sheep, 44 Purchase Street, Rye, New York 10580. Latch hooking, rya, and needlepoint.

Bon Bazar, Ltd., 149 Waverly Place, New York, New York 10014. Burlap and other backings.

Boutique Margot, 26 West 54th Street, New York, New York 10019. Needlepoint.

Canvas Patch Originals, P.O. Box 3072, Oak Ridge, Tennessee 37830. Needlepoint.

Coulter Studios, Inc., 138 East 60th Street, New York, New York 10022. Complete rya supplies: yarns, backing by the yard and prefinished for rugs, kits, color catalog, yarn cards.

Creative Canvas, Inc., 113 Main Street, Irvington, New York 10533. Needlepoint.

The Designing Woman, Lakeville, Connecticut 06039. Needlepoint.

Desiree Design Studio for Needlecrafts, Suite 122, 7942 Wisconsin Ave., Bethesda, Maryland 20014. Needlepoint.

T.E. Doelger, P.O. Box 126, Blauvelt, New York 10913. Needlepoint.

Fancywork, 1235 First Avenue, New York, New York 10021. Needlepoint.

Henry Ford Museum and Greenfield Village, Dearborn, Michigan 48121. E. S. Frost hooked rug patterns.

235

Harry M. Fraser Co., 192 Hartford Road, Manchester, Connecticut 06040. Punch hooking supplies, including hand and speed hooks, slitters, frames, backing, cloth swatches, yarn.

The Golden Eye, Box 205, Chestnut Hill, Massachusetts 02167. Needlepoint.

Greengage Designs, P.O. Box 9683, Washington, D.C. 20016. Needlepoint.

Handy Lady, 72 Garth Road, Scarsdale, New York 10583. Needlepoint and latch hooking.

Haystack, Ltd., 240 South Beverly Drive, Beverly Hills, California 90212. Needlepoint.

Frederick Herrschner Co., Hoover Road, Stevens Point, Wisconsin 54481. Needlepoint, rug backing.

Hilde's, 305 White Plains Post Road, Eastchester, New York 10709. Needlepoint and latch hooking.

Indie, 618 South Semmes, Memphis, Tennessee 38111. Needlepoint.

In Stitches, 3901 Prairie Lane, Prairie Village, Kansas 66208. Needlepoint.

The Jeweled Needle, 920 Nicollet Mall, Minneapolis, Minnesota 55402. Needlepoint.

Kaleidoscope, P.O. Box 89, Sylvania, Ohio 43560. Needlepoint.

The Knitting Needle, Armonk, New York. Needlepoint, latch hooking.

Knitting Studio, 78 Purchase Street, Rye, New York 10580. Latch hooking.

Katharine Knox, 445 Plandome Road, Manhasset, New York 11030. Needlepoint, latch hooking, punch hooking, burlap designs, monk's cloth, warp cloth, all rug yarns.

Dorothy Lawless Rug Studio, 4501 Valdina Place, Los Angeles, California 90043. Punch hooking supplies, including hooks, frames, cutters, patterns, swatches.

Lazy Daisy Needlecraft Shop, 602 East Walnut Street, Pasadena, California 91101. Needlepoint, latch hooking.

The Magic Needle, 44 Green Bay Road, Winnetka, Illinois 60093. Needlepoint.

Virginia Maxwell Custom Needlework Studio, 3404 Kirby Drive, Houston, Texas 77006. Needlepoint.

Alice Maynard, 558 Madison Avenue, New York, New York 10022. Needlepoint.

Mazaltov's, Inc., 758 Madison Avenue, New York, New York 10020 and 1980 Union Street, San Francisco, California 94123. Needlepoint.

Nantucket Needleworks, 11 South Water Street, Nantucket Island, Massachusetts 02554. Needlepoint.

Needlecraft House, West Townsend, Massachusetts 01474. Needlepoint and rya-type backing, yarns.

Needlecraft Nook, 22 Child Street, Warren, Rhode Island 02885. Latch hooking.

The Needlecraft Shop, 13561 Ventura Boulevard, Sherman Oaks, California 91403. Complete rug supplies for needlepoint, latch hooking, punch hooking, and rya, including hand and speed hookers, tufters, needles, yarn, backings.

Needlepoint à la Carte, 325 South Woodward, Birmingham, Michigan 48011. Needlepoint.

Needlepoint, Etcetera, Ltd., 408 North La Cienega Boulevard, Los Angeles, California 90048. Needlepoint.

The Needleworks, 90 East Post Road, White Plains, New York 10606. Needlepoint.

Nimble Fingers, Inc., 283 Dartmouth Street, Boston, Massachusetts 02116. Needlepoint.

The Nimble Thimble, P.O. Box 713, Aptos, California 95003. Needlepoint.

Nina Needlepoint, 860 Madison Avenue, New York, New York 10021. Needlepoint.

Norden Products, Glenview, Illinois 60025. "Eggbeater" punch hooker, frames, easels, backings, and liquid latex for punch hooking; rya-type yarn.

Papillon, 375 Pharr Road, N.E., Atlanta, Georgia 30305. Needlepoint.

Peacock Alley, 650 Croswell, S.E., Grand Rapids, Michigan 49506. Needlepoint.

Petit Point Junction, 373 North Robertson Boulevard, Los Angeles, California 90048. Needlepoint.

Pfister Associates, Torrington, Connecticut 06790. Punch hooking supplies, including hookers, slitters, frames.

The Pot Holder, 525 Warburton Avenue, Hastings-on-Hudson, New York 10706. Needlepoint, latch hooking.

The Quarter Stitch, 607 Dumaine Street, New Orleans, Louisiana 70116. Needlepoint.

Selma's Art Needlework, 1645 Second Avenue, New York, New York 10028. Needlepoint, latch hooking, rya.

The Silver Needle, Inc., 6100 Camp Bowie Boulevard, Fort Worth, Texas 76116. Needlepoint.

Sophisti-Kits, P.O. Box 5020, Pittsburgh, Pennsylvania 15206. Needlepoint.

The Textile Museum, 2320 S Street N.W., Washington, D.C. 20008. Transfer patterns of rug and textile motifs from their own and other museum collections; extensive publications.

Valley Handcrafters, Avon Park, Avon, Connecticut 06001. Needlepoint.

George Wells Rugs, Inc., 565 Cedar Swamp Road, Glen Head, Long Island, New York 11545. Punch hooking supplies, including backing materials, yarns, frames, hot iron transfer pencil, rug finishing service.

Wilson Brothers Mfg. Co., Route 8, Box 33-H, Springfield, Missouri 65804. Shuttle hooker, burlap for punch hooking.

Woolworks, 783 Madison Avenue, New York, New York 10021. Needlepoint.

Bibliography

Appleton, Le Roy H., *American Indian Design and Decoration*. New York, Dover Publications, Inc., 1971.

Bahti, Tom, *Southwestern Indian Arts and Crafts*. Flagstaff, Arizona, KC Publications, 1964.

Bennett, Ian, *Book of Oriental Carpets and Rugs*. London, Paul Hamlyn, 1972.

Bode, Wilhelm von, *Antique Rugs From the Near East*. New York, E. Weyhe, 1922.

Bowles, Ella Shannon, *Handmade Rugs*. Boston, Little, Brown & Co., 1927.

Calatchi, Robert de, *Oriental Carpets*. Rutland, Vermont, Charles E. Tuttle Co., 1967.

Campana, Michele, *European Carpets*. London, Paul Hamlyn, 1969.

Dilley, Arthur U., *Oriental Rugs and Carpets*. New York, J.B. Lippincott Co., 1959.

Encyclopedia of Needlework. New York, Hearthside Press, 1963.

Erdmann, Kurt, *Seven Hundred Years of Oriental Carpets*. Berkeley, California, University of California Press, 1970.

Faraday, Cornelia Bateman, *European and American Carpets and Rugs*. Grand Rapids, Michigan, Decorative Arts Press, 1929.

Ferrero, Mercedes, *Rugs and Tapestries from East and West*. New York, Crescent Books, 1972.

Flinders Petrie, Sir William, *Decorative Patterns of the Ancient World*. London, University College, 1930.

Turkoman Rugs. Fogg Art Museum, Cambridge, Massachusetts, Harvard University Press, 1966.

Formenton, Fabio. *Oriental Rugs and Carpets*. New York, McGraw-Hill Book Co., 1972.

Godard, Andre, *The Art of Iran.* New York, Frederick A. Praeger, 1965.

Haack, Hermann, *Oriental Rugs.* Newton, Massachusetts, Charles T. Branford, 1960.

Hackmack, Adolf, *Chinese Carpets and Rugs.* Tientsin–Peking, La Librairie Française Tientsin, 1924.

Hanley, Hope, *Needlepoint Rugs.* New York, Charles Scribner's Sons, 1971.

Hawley, Walter A., *Oriental Rugs, Antique and Modern.* New York, Dover Publications, Inc., 1970.

Hicks, Ami, *The Craft of Hand-Made Rugs.* New York, Empire State Book Co., 1936.

Hornung, Clarence P., *Treasury of American Design,* Vols. I and II. New York, Abrams, 1972.

Jacoby, Heinrich, *How to Know Oriental Carpets and Rugs.* New York, Pitman Publishing Corp. 1950.

Kahlenberg, Mary Hunt, and Berlant, Anthony, *The Navajo Blanket.* Los Angeles, Praeger Publishers, Inc. and Los Angeles County Museum of Art, 1972.

Kent, Kate Peck, *The Story of Navajo Weaving.* Phoenix, Heard Museum of Anthropology and Primitive Art, 1961.

Kent, William Winthrop, *The Hooked Rug.* New York, Dodd, Mead & Co., 1930.

———, *Hooked Rug Design.* Springfield, Massachusetts, The Pond-Ekberg Co., 1949.

———, *Rare Hooked Rugs.* Springfield, Massachusetts, The Pond-Ekberg Co., 1941.

Kirsch, Dietrich, and Kirsch-Korn, Jutta, *Make Your Own Rugs.* New York, Watson-Guptill Publications, 1969.

Landreau, Anthony N., and Pickering, W. R., *From the Bosporus to Samarkand: Flat-Woven Rugs.* Washington, D.C., The Textile Museum, 1969.

Lawless, Dorothy, *Rug Hooking and Braiding.* New York, Thomas Y. Crowell Co., 1962.

Lewis, Dr. G. Griffin, *The Practical Book of Oriental Rugs.* Philadelphia, J.B. Lippincott Co., 1920.

Liebetrau, Preben, *Oriental Rugs in Colour.* New York, The Macmillan Co., 1962.

Lorentz, H.A., *A View of Chinese Rugs.* London, Routledge & Kegan Paul Ltd., 1973.

Macbeth, Ann, *The Country Woman's Rug Book.* Peoria, Illinois, Manual Arts Press, 1929.

Marinoff, Kathryn Andrews, *Getting Started in Handmade Rugs.* New York, The Bruce Publishing Co., 1957.

Mathews, Sibyl, *Needle-Made Rugs.* New York, Hearthside Press, 1960.

McGown, Pearl, *Color in Hooked Rugs.* West Boylston, Massachusetts, 1954.

Meilach, Dona, *Making Contemporary Rugs and Wall Hangings.* New York, Abelard Schuman, 1970.

O'Brien, M., *Rug and Carpet Book.* New York, McGraw-Hill Book Co., 1946.

Pope, Arthur U., *Masterpieces of Persian Art.* New York, The Dryden Press, 1945.

Raphaelian, H.M., *The Hidden Language of Symbols in Oriental Rugs.* New Rochelle, New York, Anatol Sivas Publications, 1954.

Reed, Stanley, *All-Color Book of Oriental Carpets and Rugs.* New York, Crescent Books, 1972.

Rex, Stella, *Choice Hooked Rugs.* New York, Prentice-Hall, Inc., 1953.

Schlosser, Ignaz, *The Book of Rugs, Oriental and European.* New York, Bonanza Books, 1963.

Schürmann, Ulrich, *Oriental Carpets.* London, Paul Hamlyn, 1966.

Scobey, Joan, *Rugmaking From Start to Finish.* New York, Lancer Books, 1972.

Sides, Dorothy Smith, *Decorative Art of the Southwestern Indians.* New York, Dover Publications, Inc., 1961.

Stratton, Charlotte Kimball, *Rug Hooking Made Easy.* New York, Harper & Row. 1955.

Tattersall, C.E.C., and Reed, Stanley, *A History of British Carpets.* Leigh-in-sea, England, F. Lewis, Ltd., 1966.

Tattersall, C.E.C., *Notes on Carpet Knotting and Weaving.* London, Victoria and Albert Museum, 1920.

Weeks, Jeanne G., and Treganowan, Donald. *Rugs and Carpets of Europe and the Western World.* Philadelphia, Chilton Book Co., 1969.

Zarbock, Barbara, *The Complete Book of Rug Hooking.* New York, Van Nostrand Reinhold Co., 1961.

Znamierowski, Nell, *Step-by-Step Rugmaking* New York, Golden Press, 1972.

Index

241